THE BLUEPRINT

Why Young Offenders Need to Be Aware of Racketeering Charges

ANDRE "DRE" COOPER

NON-BINDING LEGAL INFORMATION DISCLAIMER

The author of this book, Andre D. Cooper, is not an attorney, and the material and advice reflect his own understanding of federal law. The materials in this documents/book do not constitute legal advice, are provided for general purposes only, and are not a substitute for the advice of an attorney. Thus, the author accepts no responsibility for any errors or omissions associated within this book or with any outcomes that result with the use or advice of this book and expressly disclaims any such responsibility.

Printed in the United States of America

To order additional copies of The Blue Print visit drecooperwrites.com

To all the young offenders serving them harsh sentences....

CONTENTS

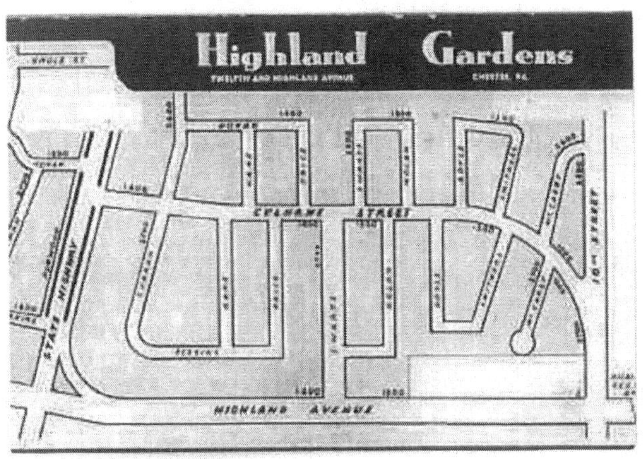

Picture of a house in highland gardens this is how the homes appeared throughout the 90s

CHAPTER 1

Stories of Chester

Do anybody think they're ready for prison? You think that you could stop everything and start a twenty-year sentence? What about dropping everything and doing a life sentence, in some of America's toughest United States Prisons? Not tough because of the convicts in them but more or so about the racist people running them. How about a death sentence where your locked away in a 6 x 9 cell, 23 hours a day, waiting to be put to death by the State or Government. None of these questions were ever explained to us, or even considered when we were growing up and out there in them streets. Why? Learning and listening to the same individuals who were never taught these things or never explained to them either. It maybe because, at the bare minimum, most of us are starting out doing crime as teenagers some even younger than that. Being told that this is just how it goes, and that in the long run crime will pay after you figure the whole hustle out. The streets have been robbing a lot of us for a long time because I guess we weren't educated properly.

A lot of people hate to hear our stories of abuse, poverty, struggles, fatherliness and motherliness homes, and sacrifice but that's cool to. I've been thinking about all of these things through 19 years of incarceration. Wondering why they let us get our hands on them drugs and pistols, and not giving us a serious discussion about the consequences of taking part in crime. Or, at the bare minimum explaining to us that dying or killing over these run-down neighborhoods and blocks which none of our families own is stupid. In addition, to explaining that the agenda of the 'Powers that Be' were for us to be forever stamped and stranded in these racist prisons. All the while getting tortured in prisons, dying in prisons, far away from our families and friends, where our lives don't matter.

My story is an example about how kids grow up to fast. So fast that nobody even has enough time to step in and slow us down. Where, most of us get caught before we can expand our thoughts and views of life. Where, the conditions, circumstances and dangerous environments shape the way we think and grow up. Places where drug dealing is just the thing to do - the inherited profession passed down - the norm, and fatal shootings and violence were nothing but a means of survival so that most could live a little longer than 18 years old. Maybe lived to see 21 years old before going to prison with a hefty sentence or getting murdered, and rarely caring about the victims of our actions.

I come from a City that had bred some of the NBA's and NFL's best, and also some of the worst of the worst criminals. This little known, and tiny area in the corner of America was named Chester by its founder William Penn.

Chester is a city in Delaware County, Pennsylvania with a population in the lower 40,000. The City sits on the western bank of the Delaware River between the cities of Philadelphia and Wilmington, Delaware but it's encircled by railroads.

Chester once served as the region's financial epicenter. In its heyday, Chester had more than 70,000 plus people living and thriving inside its border. Many of the residents had jobs on the docks or were employed at companies that paid handsome salaries such as Ford Motor Company, and Penn Shipyard. But this prosperous place came to an abrupt end like all life, physically and mentally, in Chester did. When economic hardship hit Chester - from corruption in the City's leadership and companies dissolving then leaving, the wealthy White families fled, left the poor Blacks to fend for themselves then drugs, gambling and murders soared throughout the place. I guess the crime soared due to people being neglected and racially suppressed by the Whites and America which lead to the people going into survival mode. Residents needed money, whether lawful or not, and families needed to be taking care of so the underworld of drug dealing, and gambling boomed along with the violence that put everything in to its prospective.

I was raised in the backdrop of this era. Where, the youth talked heavy and died young. And most if not all of the kids thought school was for lames, and the main goal was touching a pack and getting rich before you turned 18 years old. This was the path laid down and taught to us by Ol' Heads before any Boyle Street Boys theory came about. This was the path of Chester's youth that all of us wanted to follow and emulate it from the ones who established this foundation. It was a glorious time period for the youngsters in Chester. The illusions of driving luxury vehicles, meeting that one connect that'll change your life and homies life forever with unlimited access to truckloads of cocaine, being known for resorting to violence whenever and however, and having access to everything a teenager could imagine was vivid. This type of life held an epic hold on the youths undeveloped minds in Chester and may still do to this day. Especially, the young offenders in the Highland Gardens. This was a common route for the hustlers, savages and criminals. Nobody had sat us down, and relayed the stories of how to get the mansions and riches without crime or prison being involved. Without hurting others and causing others mothers to grieve. We were just told to sell the coke until life got better. It's crazy because the streets taught us, raised us, and failed us along with a few other adults along the way.

When I was young, in my early teens, I heard stories about the great times of Chester. At least, the stories were supposed to be great times so I thought in my undeveloped mind. These stories were about the late 60's when it was gambling that held a sway on the teenagers. The Ol' Heads use to run the stories down all the way up to the present times, in order to explain why certain people or groups in Chester had names and positions of influence.

In the late 60's, Chester was a third-class city, and under Pennsylvania's Third-Class City Code. This meant that the mayor was directly responsible for the supervision and control of the Police Department. The numbers game was where most Blacks were trying to snatch some crumbs from. Blacks and Whites worked the underworld together to a certain extent but both flourished or should I say the ones who had that forward thinking vision prospered. And, one of those legends from Chester was none other than Brother Price.

The Pennsylvania Crime Commission, State Police, and FBI labeled Willie Price as a racketeer operating in the City of Chester. Brother Price might have been named the first Black racketeer in Chester because of his close ties to organized crime figures moving around in the City. Brother Price was a boxer and had been allegedly linked to being involved in killing of a Black Muslim who he claimed broke into his home. This is what the police reports printed but the fact was that brother Price had also been a member of the Nation of Islam. Back in those days, you had some real striving members of the Nation, and also the street-slash gangsta Nation of Islam followers. So this type of outcome would have been inevitable to avoid, if it's true about his involvement. But, one thing that we know to be true is that this was normal life growing up in Chester - even back then. Brother Price had an interest in a grocery store, where it was alleged the gambling and loan sharking took place. This wasn't his only hustle. He provided loans to local residents, in order to help build the community, and dabbled in the newly flourishing drug business of Chester which had started to take a hold on the City in the early 70's. This made Brother Price a local legend, but he was also feared by many.

He had many family members on the payroll, other hustlers and gangsters in the City but one man stood out, and that was Brother David. This was Brother Price's main man when hard time called for violent times. There were also Mob ties too. Brother Price was a partner in a video poker and vending company with Joseph Iacona, who was a close associate of Santo Idone. Idone was a capo in the Bruno/Scarfo mafia family of Philadelphia and Atlantic City. Iacona was also a business partner with John Nacrelli, the former Mayor of Chester, who was more than likely the first person charged and convicted of racketeering in Chester. The second racketeering enterprise to be indicted and convicted would be members of the Bruno/Scarfo faction, and Joseph Iacona. The Boyle Street Boys, who I was charged and convicted with then sentenced to life without parole, would become the third case out of Chester. We would also be the only group that received life sentences for racketeering crimes that started when we were juveniles.

Former Mayor Nacrelli had been convicted in 1979. The conviction stemmed from his involvement with the Bruno/Scarfo crew who worked behind-the-scenes in Chester.

At the same time that the mafia was taking money out of the City of Chester, you had the other Street Kings of the

City that were talked about. Slick Rick, Cheeks, Bobby and West. They were major heroin pushers that flooded Chester, and the surrounding areas with 'New York Quarters'. This was their brand and, if you saw this on any packet of dope than you knew it was official.

As a teenager, you heard of these stories of how rich and powerful these ol' Heads were. Or, so the ones telling these stories thought that they were rich and powerful. But, these guys rode around in Cadillac Seville's, Corvettes, Porsches and Benz'. Running around the City of Chester draped in designer suits and clothes, diamonds, furs, and minks along with their beautiful females. Owning bars, stores and residential along with commercial properties. Then after them came the next crews and, or hustlers who names rang in Chester.

Asmar was one of those names. He held control of the notorious William Penn Projects in the late 80's. The rumors were back in the day that, he was one of the millionaires in Chester. Asmar had boats, Jaguars, Benz' and a Corvette. He also ran A&C Deli sandwich shop along with a trucking company in Virginia.

In or around 1988, Asmar had been charged with engaging in a Continuing Criminal Enterprise ("CCE"). This was called back than, and still is named the Kingpin statute. Asmar was the first person in Chester to be charged with such a harsh federal offense. He faced a mandatory term of life imprisonment, if convicted at a federal trial. But, Asmar later accepted a plea to a 20 year federal sentence without parole. But, Asmar was just the beginning for others to follow. You heard the stories of the legend New Years. His name was Russell Freeman, Jr. who had a female partner that once brought a mink coat worth thousands of dollars with all dollar bills of drug money. It was rumored that they were linked to or had a straight-line with some Colombians who were stationed out of Northern California. We heard the stories about Too Smallz, Darren Majid, Mitter, Pay May, D-Rock, Shams and Wali, Butch Reed, Harp, Doc Jordan and other well-known money-getters; and those other lesser known hustlers and gangsters from Chester. All of them played a part in the illusions of living a good life based on a foundation of crime. We heard of their stories from rags to riches. The struggles, and maybe violent ways to project themselves on a path to wealth. Some of them were blessed to make it, and others weren't so fortunate. For the simple reason that, it wasn't luck that got you there. You had to be ambitious, and willing to make sacrifices with your life and freedom as a down payment, in order to do the things that they were doing.

What, we weren't hearing, in detail; about were these guys fall from grace. The fact that some had money and others just knew how to portray the image of getting to a dollar. We didn't hear about the President declaring the "War on Drugs".

The harsh laws and sentences being giving to young offenders, and to some of the very men that we were idolizing. The vicious murders, home invasions, kidnappings and other violent acts being committed against some of the men family members. We didn't hear the stories of the victims families sobbing, grieving and distraught because of the lost of their loved ones.

I heard stories of these ol' Heads, as a kid from the older guys. In addition to hearing from the ol' Heads, I heard it from family members who had also fell from grace in the streets but was trying to boost my moral to achieve those so-called lofty achievements of past legends. I was never deterred from following their footsteps. Not even after experiencing my own violence, and eventual pistol-whipping, as a teenager by the hands of an adult. A known drug dealer, and killer who took revenge out on me for something that I had nothing to do with. This was just the way it was in Chester. Where, after such an act retaliation was sure to follow. But, this was also an act that turned my heart cold, ugly, and scarred that day.

CHAPTER 2

Product of the Environment

I still remember like it was yesterday. This vivid memory has haunted me, in a number of ways. Some in positive ways, and other times negatively but the experience has made a lasting impact nonetheless on my overall well-being. Basically, turning me in to a product of the environment.

The hulk was stalking through the menacing dark streets of Chester. Especially, on the tiny streets of Nolan and Perkins that lay inside of the Highland Gardens neighborhood.

Nolan Street was a long and narrow, one-way, block that had about twenty, rundown, row homes on it. The residential styled homes had small gates, may be 3 feet, with even smaller front yards. Some homes, if you wanted to call them that, had grass; others had little patches of grass while others had straight brown, finely powder, grimy looking dirt. The area wasn't a pretty site on the strip. Nolan Street stopped at a Stop sign where it connected to Perkins Street that provided an one-way lane on to Swartz Street. Swartz Street lead out of the Highland Gardens neighborhood on to a two-way street called Highland Avenue. Where, a housing project named McCafferty Village stood grim across the street.

The tiny streets were gloom from its appearance. Abandon homes, littered yards with trash, and grass providing the backdrop. This didn't include the fact that several violent crimes such as murders and tons of drugs among other things had occurred on the street throughout the existence of its time.

The November wind blew hard and heavy. It tossed chip bags, tiny plastic glassine bags, sandwich bags with marijuana and cocaine residue still in them. Other little trash and debris flew also that the hulk blew across the grassless yards. Some trash stuck to fences while a few others traveled on the cold street. It sort of resemble an old Western movie. Where the cactus blows across the lifeless and barren desert, but Nolan and Perkins Streets were different from any Hollywood movie set or barren desert, and none of this stopped us though.

I leaned up against the corner house. The house where the Stop sign had been placed in the dusty yard by the City of Chester. The house or home, if you wanted to call this dilapidated place that. It more or so resembled an abandoned home from the outside, with the lights on and some dirty windows still intact, but it wasn't. With the dusty front and backyards, broken down vehicles parked in both, and dirty white front doors; the place belonged to a friend of mine who went by the name of T-Bone. He lived there with his parents, brother, slew of cousins, and a black Lab that everybody called - Dollar. Dollar was a vicious street dog that had been through just as many battles as the residents who lived in the Highland Gardens.

It was the typical environment that we all grew up in. But, what separated this place from my home was that this is where a lot of the action went down at. You had a few other spots in the neighborhood that were used to sell drugs, but this was where it was at for this time-period. The block dubbed "Boyle Street Boys" wouldn't be functioning full throttle until a few years later. The older guys or ol' Heads, as we called them in Chester, hung around the corner on a street named Culhane but everybody around the way called it the Block or Cocaine Street. But, this corner section of Nolan and Perkins was my tiny world, at the time until everybody around the neighborhood started splitting the blocks up. This place was dubbed the Cut-Off by a few young hustlers who founded it. This was where all the young hustlers gravitated to, so that we could cut-off the drug money before it got to the Block.

My two friends who were also in their early teens, Tate and Moe, stood up against a grey Oldsmobile that had tinted windows and chrome basket rims on it. It was their car. They had just purchased the vehicle a few days ago and were pulling an all-nighter trying to make the paper back. They were propped against the car passing a Dutch Master back-and-forth while I stood a few feet away, sandwiched between two broken vehicles parked in the yard, up the little hill next to T-Bone's dirty house door.

"Yo, let me hit that!" I said, before heading down towards them. I had on an all black Nautica coat, black jeans and black low-top Timberland boots called Chuckka's with a black skull cap on. All that could be seen on me was the beardless, round, brown face. I was fifteen years old, and this was 1995.

"Man, its cold as shit out here... Let's jump in the car and smoke." Moe said and moved around to the driver's side door but didn't get in the car. He had on an outfit similar to mines except he wore a black Polo jacket. Moe stood 5'6, weighed 140 pounds, and he was only 15 years old.

Tate passed the Dutch to me then went to check his beeper that had just went off. He also had all black on, and wore a black, puffy; NorthFace coat. Tate was a year older than us, at 16 years old but stood 5'9 than weighed 170 pounds. A big boy for his age. "I got to make a sell around Park Terrace... Come on..." He stated to us after checking his beeper.

"Y'all go' head... I got to take the car back." I responded.

"We go'in to pick you up then go around the spot, after I make the sell." Tate replied while getting into the passenger side of the Oldsmobile.

"Take the jawn wit you to walk back up the way." Tate said, while pulling out a black snub-nose 38 Special from his right-side coat pocket.

"Nah, I'm aight... Just swing back through to grab me because its cold ass shit out here."

"Right!"

I stepped out of the yard then headed to the row of parked cars on Perkins Street. My Mother's burgundy Buick was parked at the top of the street. I slide in the driver side of the Buick then turned it on. Nas' song Street Dreamz came blasting through the stereo system. I hit the Dutch a few times while bobbing my head then flicked the heat all the way up on blast.

I finished the Dutch then rolled all the windows down in the car. I needed to air it out before taking the car home. The crisp night air filled the Buick and provided a little relief from the marijuana stench that my Mother hated so badly.

I yanked off the block and out of the Highland Gardens. My Mother had just moved out of the neighborhood but not far enough. We had moved around the corner to a different neighborhood that was kind of laid back. A few white people lived on the street but were in the process of leaving the area. The homes were much better than the ones in the Highland Gardens and didn't come with all the mice and roaches. But, the one thing that wasn't good about the spot is that the McCafferty Housing Projects sat five blocks behind it.

It took less than five minutes to make it to the house. I parked in front of the home then rolled the windows up. But, before I got out of the car I lit a Newport up.

Out of the corner of my eye, I seen a dark figure sitting on the steps on my Mom's house. I turned to get a better view and realized who it was.

I leaped out of the vehicle then strolled up the sidewalk to the house. My Uncle Stone was sitting on the steps smoking a Newport. He was dressed in all black, and scheming, I guess. Stone's eyes were glassy, and he smelled of liquor. "Hun put these in the crib for Mom-Mom..." I said, while walking towards him with the car keys in my hand.

"I thought you were taking care of something tonight?" Stone responded.

It was something we did. We both took turns keeping the car out at night, at least until I got my own car a few months later. Even though, I was fifteen years old and riding around with pistols in the car, it was 2:00am at night and I didn't have a driver's license. This didn't matter at all. I was already grown by this time. At least, in my little teenaged mind, and the overall scheme of things in Chester.

"Nah... I'ma pull an all nighter, and I'm not trying to be coming back tak'in Mom-Mom to work in the morn'in."

"You go'in be up anyway... You might as well take her to work in the morn'in."

"Nah Unc, I ain't try'in to be do'in all that... You do it..." I said then threw him the keys.

"You put gas in the jawn?"

"I ain't go nowhere but up the way."

"I'ma take you back up the way... Hold up..."

"I'm cool... I'ma walk up there." I replied before turning around and heading up the walk-way.

"You got a jawn on you?" Stone asked trying to make sure that I was safe and carrying a weapon.

"Yeah!" I lied then headed up the street.

I moved down the semi-dark street. The only thing that brought some sort of light to the street was the dealership which sat across from the house. We lived right across the street from Murphy Ford, and the dealership had a nice-size lot worth of cars and trucks everywhere. So, in order to avoid all the breaking-in and stealing of the vehicles, they had flooded the lot with lights. I reached the bottom of the street then started walking pass the old elementary school called William Penn. The school was named after the so-called founder of Pennsylvania. I had once attended the school, as a kid. On the other side of the street was the back of the McCafferty Projects. A large field with a basketball court, and an old baseball field that the two, separated the side-walks; and Projects from me.

I reached in my pocket then pulled another Dutch out. I tried to spark it up, but the lighter kept going out due to the wind blowing hard. I tried again and again then a fifth time.

I stopped moving then used one hand to cover the Dutch with.

I lit the Dutch up then took a heavy pull. By this time, I was at the end of six-foot gate where it stopped and reached another part of the Project's. I glanced up, out of pure instincts and seen a black figure leaning on the side of the Project building. I didn't pay it no mind, so I continued to walk. *As* I got closer to the crowded parking lot full of vehicles, the black figure started to become clearer to me. I thought about crossing the street but decided not to. That would've been a stupid move, so I headed forward and decided to face my worst fears. But, I intended to be tough and not appear scared or vulnerable. My goal was on trying to bluff the would-be stick-up kid. Normally, this worked - sometimes. Most stick-up boys didn't want to rob a person who would put up a fight, or even pull a gun out on them. If you appeared strapped than you were good. So, I slide my hand down towards the waist and underneath of the coat.

The black figure stood on the side of the building waiting patiently. The Projects were old. It was built back in the early 60's for low-income or damn near poor or outright poor Black folks of Chester to live in. The buildings were only two-stories high, and dark orange in color but stood out none-the-less to remind you of what exactly they were.

This was the government's main attractions in Black communities. Anywhere in America you went and came across these types of structures or buildings than you knew exactly what they were and who lived in them.

I got closer to the black figure. My eyes almost popped out because they couldn't believe what I saw. A tall older, pitch black, man who had a black bullet-proof vest on with no shirt, black jeans and boots. I knew who he was from being in the mix of the streets, even at this young age. He was a cold-hearted gangsta who sold a lot of drugs and known to kill. I heard rumors of his work and had a lot of respect for him - up until this moment. He darted out from off the side of the building and headed towards me. A long silver handgun was in the right-hand, and he pointed it directly at my head.

"Damn!" I said, only to myself. My instincts had told me to cross the street or run, but my little fifteen-year-old, Chester tuff ego, said not too. I couldn't show no weakness. I knew he was a killer, and the first site of weakness than I was dead. This is just how it was in the streets. Especially, for most murderers, after that first killing. They be feigning for that feeling of power and strength of pulling the trigger.

"Come here!.. you b!&P# a$$ N!**!" He stated then grabbed me by the coat. He swung the huge 9mm at the same time, as he gripped me by the collar.

"Boom!!!" The semi-automatic weapon went off, as it hit the upper part of my face by the eye. I leaned over a little bit.

"Damn, this n!**! just rock'ed me... Am I dead'?" I thought to myself, as he yanked my 110-pound frame towards him.

I was smacked in the face three more times, but the gun didn't go off. At that point, from the smacks and pain, I knew that I was still alive.

"Where the rest of the buls at?"

"What?" I asked, faintly.

"Where the rest of ya buls at?" He yelled while dragging me, at gun point, deeper into the Project's.

I didn't know what he was talking about. "What n!**!!" I got smacked again with the gun. By this time, I was being lead across another parking lot which sat directly across from the Highland Gardens. Highland Avenue separated the two neighborhoods and acted like neutral grounds for the two neighborhoods who have been rival enemies since the beginning of time. A beef that nobody to this day can trace back to any significant incident, disrespectful act or murder of a family or friend. Maybe, in the present, some of the people on both sides can but not back then. I fell to the ground from the blow to the head and tried again to regain my senses. I heard a car race up and door open. My face was covered in blood. I could barely see but I heard another figure running over.

"This the p#$$4! This him! Let me hit him!"

I rolled over and seen another man standing over top of me. He had all black clothing on but wore a black ski-mask to hide his identity. An all-black Tech-9, with the banana clip hanging out, was in his hand and pointed it directly at me. I balled up then squirmed from side-to-side, and he adjusted his aim with every move that I made. "Nah! Nah! Nah!" I yelled while in a ball and squirming trying to avoid getting shot in the head or stomach.

"Not right here!" No Shirt said. He snatched me up, at gunpoint, then we marched through the dark Project's alleyway.

We stumbled pass a few buildings then on the side of a dark alleyway. At that moment, I thought they were going to slump me than leave my body in the gutter for the police to find but this didn't happen. They had another plan for me.

The alleyway lead to another, dark street named Pine Lane. A red, four-door, car sat double-parked in the street.

The back door on the driver's side popped out. "Pop the trunk!" No Shirt yelled, as we approached the car.

The trunk flew up then No Shirt tried to drag me to it. "Get the f*Win!" I start pulling away and trying to get out of his grip. I had made up my mind in the alleyway that the first chance I got to run that I was going to take that chance. They would have to shot me while running. I wasn't going to make it easy for them no more, and definitely wasn't getting in the truck.

"No! No I'm not getting in the trunk!" I yelled.

I know how it would've ended, if I got into the trunk. There was no way that I was getting into it freely. Getting in the trunk meant death, and I wasn't going to let them kill me that easy. They were going to have to work hard for this kill.

The second guy with the Tech-9 spoke. "Put him in the car!"

No Shirt yanked hard then threw me in the back seat while he got in the front. Tech-9 sat next to me with the gun trained towards my stomach. He still had the mask on. "Try somethin stupid, and I'll rock you."

My face was smothered in blood and sweat. I could only see out of one eye. I had all type of thoughts running through my head. "What to do!? What to do!?" I started thinking, in panic mood. I had just did the stupidest thing by getting in the car. Now, instead of two killers, there was another man driving the car. I glanced up then looked his way.

The driver turned around to see who the killers had caught. This was at the same time that I glanced to take a peek at him. The driver seen me and couldn't believe what he saw. We were both young boys and cool who knew each other from being around the city. This didn't help though. He couldn't go against his ol' Heads. This was just how it was.

"Pull off young bul! Pull off!" The driver yanked off and drove down the street. He made a right turn on 12th street.

I sat in the back seat, alert but in deep thought, trying to put a plan together. My thoughts were interrupted by a child's scream.

"Damn, I thought the jawn had jammed until I smacked this n!$$*..." No Shirt said, to the others while turned sideways staring at me. He was playing with the gun, and aimed directly at my head..

A loud scream then cry rung out again. "Ssss... It's go'in to be aight!" No Shirt stated to his son, as he turned around to console the little boy who was curled up under the passenger side dash board.

I stared directly at the little boy who appeared no older than 3 years old. Tears were falling from his eyes, and he appeared terrified. My head shook from side-to-side. At that moment, I knew that I was getting murdered if I didn't think of something to do. This whole ordeal was bigger than me, at least I thought. I still didn't know what was going on.

The car stormed down 12th Street then stopped in the middle of the Project's. I glanced up then out of the window to see what was going on, and whether or not I could escape. The place was packed at 2:30 in the morning. You had people in the street, on sidewalks, in between the dark buildings; and others staring out of their 2nd floor windows.

"Pull over! Pull over!" No Shirt ordered.

He pulled the car over. They all leaped out of the car then No Shirt came, and yanked me out by the collar. "I caught one of those Garden buls right here... He act'in like he don't know what's go'in on.... I'ma make'em remember though."

No Shirt said, about to smack me again with the gun until somebody yelled.

"5-0! 5-0!"

No Shirt stuck the pistol in my back then whispered, "you try anything and I'ma kill you and that cop."

I didn't move. I knew that he was serious, and meant exactly that. Killing both of us. Right here in the middle of the Project's in front of millions. All just to make a point. So, I stood there as the Police cruiser drove, slowly, through the Project street. The Officer glanced around the area. It was close to 300 hundred people out there. They were drunk, high and armed to the teeth. He wasn't pulling over at this time of the night to see why all these people were loitering.

The Officer stared over towards our way, so I tried to turn my head a little, in order to show the bloody face. No Shirt nudged me in the back with the gun. The Officer continued to drive down 12th street then turned on to Highland Avenue.

"Who y'all got up there? Who dat! Is it one of those Garden buls?" A heavy-set, brown skin, drunken man said, while stumbling up to us.

"I got one of those n!$$@!" No Shirt replied.

The drunk got closer. I didn't bother to stare at him. My mind was racing still on how to make a dash for it. Or do anything possible to get away from these cold-hearted killers. I had too. The savages had me on display like a wounded animal begging for help or death to stop the torture.

The man stepped towards me. He had a 40oz bottle of Old English in one hand, and a Newport in the other. "Yo, he a youngbul... Youngbul, you had someth'in to do wit try'in to grab my man?"

The voice had sounded familiar, so I glanced up to see who it was. "Damn, Dre!" Was all the man could say, as he turned his head when he seen my bloody and distorted face.

"Nah Pozz, come on man, you know me. I didn't have nothing to do wit that!" I stated with certainty, and belief that the ol'Head would believe me.

I couldn't believe the effect my face had on him but I used it to my advantage. I embraced the moment. "Come on, ol' Head, you know me!" I stated again.

Pozz was a well-known figure in the Project's. He had those days back in the 80's of trying to get to a dollar, and all of the other nonsense that came with the street life. But, Pozz always loved the kids and tried to get them to do better than he had done in life. Especially, if you had some basketball skills.

We had meant when I was 9 or 10 years old on the basketball court. McCafferty Village had a playground in the middle of the Project's, and I use to hang over there with my cousins. One day, after-school, Pozz and a few others put together a three-on-three basketball tournament. It was an unexpected tournament, and all of the drug dealers, hustlers, and gangsters were placing bets on certain teams. Pozz had bet on the team that I played on because his little brother was on the team. Pozz liked how we played together. We won the tournament. After the games, Pozz asked me to play on his Summer League team. I agreed to play, even though it was mainly boys from the Project's on the team. The Summer games came, and on the first day a fight broke out. Shots rang out next then a person got killed. (He's still doing a life without parole sentence for that murder. At least to my knowledge because I think the guy was like 18 or 19 years old.) This event was the end of the basketball tournament in Memorial Park. I always remained friends with Pozz, as I got older. He knew that I loved to play ball, mess with the girls, and sell drugs.

Pozz started shaking his head, "Y'all got the wrong bul! Nah! Nah! Dre ain't in to dat!"

"What!" No Shirt stated.

"Nah, Dre wouldn't do dat... Would you?" He asked while everybody stared.

Pozz knew that I didn't have any thing to do with trying to kidnap No Shirt, and his son. At least not the "Dre" that he knew from those basketball days. "You know me better than dat - Pozz... I'm not into that..."

"Nah, Dre ain't do dat... He youngbul.. Y'all got to let'em go, man..." Pozz stated, and kept saying that to get the attention off of me.

"Who the f*ck$ did it?" No Shirt asked again but in a way, as if he was trying to read me. You know the eyes don't lie. He wanted to see whether or not I really had something to do with it. Growing up in these types of environments you had to be able to read people's actions and moods to survive. No matter what age you were. "I don't know... I'm just com'in from the crib..."

"Let'em go... Dre don't have noth'in to do wit it..." Pozz stated again trying to convince No Shirt. No Shirt gave an ice cold stare while thinking about what to do. It seemed like a whole hour went by before he stated, "get outtta here."

I spent to the right then speed walked down 12th street which took you down to Highland Avenue. It wasn't a far walk. The Highland Gardens, and a store that everybody hung at named DeMarco's was in site. I didn't even think for a second to thank Pozz for the help. I needed to get out of the Project's, and away from the hostile crowd.

My mind was racing, and all I thought about was getting No Shirt. He knew I was young and didn't have nothing to do with the attempted kidnapping.

DeMarco's came in to full-view, as I made it out of McCafferty Village. I turned then stared back at the large crowd still gathered around No Shirt.

I turned back around then dashed across Highland Avenue, past DeMarco's then up the alleyway towards Perkins Street. I needed to get my hands on a gun, and fast. When I made it back up the street, I banged on T-Bone's door. Dollar started barking then T-Bone swung the door open. "Damn! Ya jawn twisted..." He stated when seeing my face.

"Where Tate and Moe?"

"They went over there try'in to get you back.. Somebody stormed up here talk'in 'bout they trunk'ed you." He stated then turned in to the house. I followed behind T-Bone then took a seat on the dusty couch.

"Who told y'all they grabbed me?"

"The bul and them who tried to grab the bul."

"Who!" I asked again.

"You know who be grabb'in buls up here."

"Yo, let men see ya jawn real quick!"

"I just gave them it... They went over there two cars deep for you."

"Damn!" I said then laid back on the couch. My head started throbbing, and blood covered my face. I didn't bother to clean it or take any medicine or go to the hospital. My adrenaline was still pumping. Revenge ran through the veins. My heart turned cold, and determined to make No Shirt and them feel the same pain.

"Hun..." T-Bone said, as he handed me the Dutch.

From that moment forward I vowed to be the wolf and not the sheep. Basically, I was going to be a product of my environment. I wasn't choosing to be a victim. Life had a way of making a person decide important things like being a victim or not. A criminal or not. A boy or man. All of these things were questions kids, teenagers, juveniles or what ever you wanted to call them were asked at a young age without all the necessary information or skills to make an informed choice to do the right thing, in any of the above circumstances. A lot of pressure for any individual at any point in their life.

This was my introduction to physical violence being committed against me, so that's why I'm not ashamed to relay the story. It may help the next person survive a moment like this or deter them from this type of life period. But, what this incident also did was played a major part on why the way I moved on the streets growing up. It's not an excuse, at least on the surface, but it holds substantial weight on why young offenders, like myself, committed violent crimes growing up.

BOYLE ST. BOYS DEFENSE:

WHY THEY KILLED

Chester's culture of corruption and crime fingered as culprit

The drug-dealing Boyle Street Boys hold the Highland Gardens section of Chester in a grip of fear.

ANDRE COOPER

JAMAIN WILLIAMS

Page 3

An article that appeared in the Daily News Paper during our trial.

CHAPTER 3

Federal Crimes

I think of that pistol-whipping often. Not with the mindset of revenging that disrespectful act but often thinking this is where the turning-point in my life happened. Years later I would be the aggressor by pistol-whipping a few others who were involved in the drug trade, shooting a few people, and numerous other crimes against people. Just to be certain, this is nothing that I am proud of or intend to glorify but this is the reality of growing up in those types of environments. I wouldn't advise any other youngster to follow this path. For the simple reason that, the choice to commit violence can land a person in a place that I currently live at and will potentially die at -- Federal prison. But, don't get me wrong, I don't advocate people being victims either.

It doesn't even make sense that, by the age of 15 years old, I had already been shot at several times; involved in a lot of drug activity, seen shoot-outs, people being murdered; and all the other things that teenagers go through in them poverty-stricken environments.

As I said before that pistol-whipping was different for me. More importantly though, this incident happened right before the Government stated that I played a part in forming or being recruited in a drug conspiracy/racketeering enterprise. It all depends on who testimony at trial you want to believe.

When hearing the stories about them old legends, I never knew that having less than two people who brought and sold cocaine could be labeled a major drug trafficking organization. Major drug trafficking conspiracies and racketeering were two terms that I had never heard of at the age of 16 years old. I don't think no teenager could grasp this type of sophisticated concept, and let alone form either of the two things for any illegal purposes. But, that's not what the Government thought. The Government came up with this conclusion because of Mafia prosecutions under RICO, and these cases started developing around the 1980's. Following these successful prosecutions of the Mob figures including the ones out of the City of Chester, the Department of Justice came up with some internal guidelines to adhere to so that the RICO statute wasn't broadly used against just anybody or group.

The procedure begins when prosecutors at United States Attorney's Offices throughout the nation prepare proposals outlining prospective RICO prosecutions and

submit them to the Organized Crime and Racketeering Section at the DOJ for approval. DOJ will not prosecute a case under RICO unless it meets at least one or more of the following prosecution guidelines:

1. RICO is necessary to ensure that the indictment adequately reflects the nature and extent of the criminal conduct involved in a way that prosecution only on the underlying charges would not;
2. RICO prosecution would provide the basis for an appropriate sentence under all of the circumstances of the case;
3. RICO charge could combine related offenses which would otherwise have to be prosecuted separately in different jurisdictions;
4. RICO is necessary for a successful prosecution of the Government's case against the defendant or a co-defendant;
5. use of RICO would provide a reasonable expectation of forfeiture which is proportionate to the underlying criminal conduct;
6. the case consists of violations of state law, but local law enforcement officials are unlikely or unable to

successfully prosecute the case, in which the federal government has a significant interest;

7. the case consists of violations of state law, but involves prosecution of significant Political or government individuals, which may pose special problems for the local prosecutor. **(ORGANIZED CRIME AND RACKETEERING SECTION, U.S. DEPT OF JUSTICE, RACKETEER INFLUENCED AND CORRUPT ORGANIZATIONS(RICO): A MANUAL FOR FEDERAL PROSECUTORS 128 (2d ed. 1988)**

Although, I do not know for sure, if the Government went through these procedures to arrest me. They may have but I couldn't tell you which one of these guidelines that the "Boyle Street Boys" fell under to be prosecuted federally.

I was indicted in February of 2003 at the age of 23 years old. The indictment stated that I was part of a violent cocaine racketeering enterprise which started in or around the years of 1996 and lasted all the way up until December of 2002. Three fatal shootings occurred through this time-period that I am charged with under the 'Violent Crimes in Aid of Racketeering' federal offense - 18 USC §1959(a)(1).

I was 16 years old at the start of this Racketeering and cocaine (drug) trafficking enterprise and, so were most of my co-defendants. Nobody was over the age of 17 years old when the enterprise was supposed to be thought of and formed, and agreements to commit murder and other violent criminal acts were formed. They're saying that we came up with this idea, as teenagers. But, the Government arrested us in our early twenties.

The evidence adduced at trial indicated that several others, and I intersected and intertwined our personal relationships together and formed an association or drug enterprise called, the "Boyle Street Boys". We all grew up in the same run-down place and were childhood friends.

While the majority of us were youth, as the indictment and evidence at trial stated and the Government stated in their opening and closing arguments but this group or enterprise was anything less than organized and together.

I was also charged with aiding and abetting a federal witness murder, in violation of the Tampering With A Witness statute, and under the 'Violent Crimes In Aid of Racketeering'. I got charged two ways with this fatal shooting. In addition, I was charged with aiding and abetting another murder of a member of the conspiracy. This offense was also charged under the VICAR statute. And, the Federal Government charged me with killing another 19 year old. This is the federal offense that says that I actually killed someone, and charged me under the

VICAR statute. I had turned 20 years old in June of 1999, and the murder occurred on July 1999. They used the evidence of a drug conspiracy and racketeering enterprise to convict me on this murder, as well as all the other fatal shootings. Specifically, the accusation says that the murder I'm charged with personally committing happened over drugs but evidence at trial says that the murder was over the other person killing my cousin who was also 23 years old when he got murdered.

All of the violence that I'm convicted of occurred either at the age of 21 years old or younger.

Unfortunately though, the manner in which I was indicted and tried made the convictions a pre-ordained conclusion for us. Charges that were not related were joined, we were tried to a death-qualified and anonymous jury, and all manner of irrelevances were permitted under the guise of co-conspirator statements and evidence of conspiracy.

To make a long story short, me and another co-defendant went to the death penalty phase of my trial. The jury did not vote for death. This occurred by the grace and mercy of the Most High then the skin of my teeth. The vote was 11-1 for death.

I'm not on death row because the lawyers explained that I grew up in a drug infested and violent city, and household. I was treated unfairly by the judicial system and sent to spend the rest of my life in federal maximum security prisons around the Country. I 've been to a bunch of them around the Country too. I say unfairly because we were youth or young offenders who never knew any other way to survive. Our brains weren't fully-developed throughout this time-period. Which, now, the professors and experts have studied and stated that -- yes, your still not grown at 21 years old.

In between the years of 2005 and 2016, the United States Supreme Court issued several landmark decisions that profoundly alter the status and treatment of youth in the justice system. Construing the Eighth Amendment, the Court held in Roper v Simmons that juveniles are sufficiently less blameworthy than adults, such that the application of different sentencing principles were required under the Eighth Amendment, even in cases of capital murder. In Graham v. Florida, the Court, seeing no meaningful distinction between death or life without parole, found that the Eighth Amendment categorically prohibited life without parole sentences for non-homicide crimes for juveniles.

Then, Miller v. Alabama, the United States Supreme Court held that the Eighth Amendment forbids a sentencing scheme that mandates life in prison without the possibility of parole for juvenile offenders." Justice Kagan, writing for the majority, was explicit in articulating the Court's rationale: the mandatory imposition of life without parole sentences "prevents those meting out punishment from considering a juvenile's 'lessened culpability' and greater 'capacity for change,' and runs afoul of our cases 'requirement of individualized sentencing for defendants facing the most serious penalties.'" The Court grounded its holding "not only on common sense.., but on science and social science as well," all of which demonstrate fundamental differences between the juveniles and adults.

The Court in Miller noted the scientific "findings - of transient rashness, proclivity for risk, and inability to assess consequences - both lessened a child's 'moral culpability' and enhanced the prospect that, as the years go by and neurological development occurs, his 'deficiencies will be reformed'. Importantly, the Court specifically found that none of what Graham "said about children - about their distinctive (and transitory) mental traits and environmental vulnerabilities - is crime specific." Relying on Graham, Roper and other previous decisions on individualized sentencing, the Court held "that in imposing a State's harshest penalties, a sentencer misses too much if he treats every child as an adult." The Court also emphasized that a young offender moral failings could not be comparable to an adult's because there is a stronger possibility of rehabilitation.

Despite all of this evidence, guidance, and scientific reports - federal courts around the Country have been reluctant to apply these principles to young offenders who were teens when the drug conspiracy or RICO enterprises were formed. I know this to be the case because I tried to receive relief from these life sentences that I received. The Court of Appeals out of the Eastern District of Pennsylvania in Philadelphia denied relief. The Appeals Court never even considered the question of a person entering in to the drug conspiracy, as a teenager then continuing in this illegal activity until being caught in their mid 20's. But, other federal courts, and the Government were denying you relief because of a term named - Ratification. A legal term that I'll explain further later on. There were a few federal courts that are outliers on this issue. Maybe one or two that I found. The District of Columbia Circuit Court of Appeals applied Miller to a defendant who began conspiring to commit his instant crime while under age then completed the crime upon reaching adulthood. Andre Williams was convicted of his role in a conspiracy to participate in a racketeer influenced corrupt organization ("RICO") and to distribute illegal drugs. Williams was active in 'the conspiracy from 1983 to 1991 but did not turn 18 until 1987. Andre Williams had been 13 years old when entering into the RICO conspiracy. Unbelievable! However, years later the D.C. Court of Appeals sent his case back to the district court. Instead of the Government arguing that Miller didn't apply to Williams they agreed to a reduced sentence of 30 years. Andre Williams received immediate release, and went on to prosper post-release. I know these facts because I spent a few years with his brother and other co-defendant who also entered this RICO conspiracy as teenagers but did not get the same sentence reduction that Andre Williams received. This is just purely wrong. I thought that, justice was equal around the board.

At least, this is what we are taught. Nope! I was fed up with this lopsided justice being given out by the federal courts so I decided to go on a writing campaign about it. In June of 2019, I wrote an article named - Who's Going to Save Us! Here's the complete essay that I wrote:

Who's Going to Save Us!

On behalf of all the juveniles and young adolescent lifers in America, but more importantly in the federal system, why has not the Washington legislators taken action. Why has not the legislators taken action to protect its youth and young adolescents from draconian sentences we're currently serving - life without the possibility of parole? A punishment that buries us alive in the federal penal system. Punishments handed out, based on juvenile and young adolescent conduct when our brains are not fully developed and we're still vulnerable to follow others, and subject to peer pressure to commit violent acts or any stupid juvenile act without thinking twice about the consequences of harming others or being harmed.

It's amazing. Or maybe it's just the norm, now, how once again the criminal justice system is showing Americans, and the world alike, that it has a two-tiered system of justice. I state this fact because of the truth of the matter, and for the simple fact that I recently came across several articles and advertisements that were trying to push the 'Tobacco 21' movement. There're two bills out there but I came across the one by two well-known legislators. Senators Mitch McConnell(R-Ky) and Tim Kane(D-Va) introduced a bill on May 20, 2019 called the Tobacco-Free Youth Act. Which is designed to address the "public health crisis" of teen e-cigarette use. This is an admiral bill no doubt, and is a significant cause to be part of and to help those teens who's brains prefrontal cortex, which controls judgments and impulse, is still growing and maturing during the teenage years, well way up until the mid-20's. Why has not a similar bill been introduced for juveniles and young adolescent lifers between the ages of 18-25 years old? The same studies by some of the most distinguished professors from Harvard, Yale, Columbia and Temple University, on juvenile brain maturity, were used by legislators to come up with the 'Tobacco 21' bill.

Why can't juveniles and young adolescent lifers receive a similar bill in order to save us from this draconian sentence? For the simple reason that the studies apply to our cause also, and there were once procedures and constitutional protections for juveniles and young adolescents being sentenced in federal courts. A short time before the war on drugs took shape, and the excessive sentences practices in the late 80's and early 90's started to take hold of the federal judicial system, there were federal statutes in effect called the "Federal Youth Corrections Act" and "Young Adult Offenders Act." In the Youth Corrections Act, the statute had defined a youth offender as "a person under the age of twenty-two at the time of convictions" 18 USC §5006(d). Convicted persons between the ages of twenty-two and twenty-six are termed "young adult offenders" and may be sentenced for treatment under YCA if the sentencing court "finds that there are reasonable grounds to believe that the defendant will benefit from the treatment provided under the Federal Youth Corrections Act, 18 USC §4216. These statutes provided sentencing procedures for juveniles and young adolescents between the ages of 18-25 years old but focused more on whether the juvenile or young adolescent was subject to be reformed. These statutes were abolished by the "Sentencing Reform Act of 1984." The Sentencing Reform Act of 1984 contained in the Comprehensive Crime Control Act of 1984, dramatically changed the federal sentencing. Until then, trial judges had a good deal of discretion regarding sentences to be imposed after the defendant was convicted of a criminal offense. Under the act, federal sentences were determined based on a combination of mandatory minimum sentences and mandatory guideline sentencing schemes. I think, the general legislators need to reconsider these statutes along with the newly available scientific findings by the distinguished experts in the field of brain research, and bring back some much needed juvenile and young adolescent reform. Clearly the Supreme Court is headed in that direction but are falling short in one aspect. The Supreme Court has limited relief to those juveniles under 18 years old. Why? It doesn't make sense, if the High Court is viewing the same research and expert studies, which we know that they are.

In between the years of 2005 and 2016, the United States Supreme Court issued several landmark decisions that profoundly alter the status and treatment of youth in the justice system. Construing the Eighth Amendment, the Court in Roper v. Simmons that juveniles are sufficiently less blameworthy than adults, such that the application of different sentencing principles is required under the Eighth Amendment, even in cases of capital murder. In Graham v. Florida, the Court, seeing no meaningful distinction between a sense of death or life without parole, found that the Eighth Amendment categorically prohibited life without parole sentences for non-homicide crimes for juveniles.

Then, in Miller v. Alabama, the United States Supreme Court held "that the Eighth Amendment forbids a sentencing scheme that mandates life in prison without the possibility of parole for juvenile offenders." Justice Kagan, writing for the majority, was explicit in articulating the Court's rationale: the mandatory imposition of life without parole sentences "prevents those meting out punishment from considering a juvenile's 'lessened culpability' and greater 'capacity for change,' and runs afoul of our cases 'requirement of individualized sentencing for defendants facing the most serious penalties." The Court grounded its holding "not only on common sense.., but on science and social science as well," all of which demonstrate fundamental differences between the juveniles and adults.

The Court in Miller noted the scientific "findings - of transient rashness, proclivity for risk, and inability to assess consequences -both lessened a child's 'moral culpability' and enhanced the prospect that, as the years go by and neurological development occurs, his 'deficiencies will be reformed.' Importantly, the Court specifically found that none of what Graham "said about children - about their distinctive (and transitory) mental traits and environmental vulnerabilities - is crime specific." Relying on Graham, Roper and other previous decisions on individualized sentencing, the Court held "that in imposing a State's harshest penalties, a sentencer misses too much if he treats every child as an adult." The Court also emphasized that a young offender's moral failings could not be comparable to an adult's because there is a stronger possibility of rehabilitation.

Thus, the Supreme Court is begging the legislature to chime in on the conversation. But, the Washington lawmakers have not and remained silent on the juvenile and young adolescent issues for some time now. The federal legislators have remained silent, even when several states around the country are recognizing the difference in juvenile and young adolescent brains' slow-growth and immaturity.

California, Illinois, Vermont and the District of Columbia are just a few. Moreover, in the District of Columbia there is a current bill pending titled, "The Second Look Amendment Act of 2019," where the Courts would be allowed to take a second look at defendants with life sentences and the equivalent of a life sentence, that committed crimes between the ages of 18-25 years old with twenty years of imprisonment done. This is a start in the right direction to help stem the mass incarceration. But what about the federal legislators?

At the current moment, there is nothing for juveniles and young adolescents like myself pending in either houses of the lawmakers in Washington. In addition to no bills pending on the juveniles and young adolescents, nobody is asking the presidential contenders their stances on the juveniles and young adolescent issue either. Well, could President Trump help? I don't know because nobody has brought this to the President's attention. Maybe I'll be the first juvenile/young adolescent offender to ask the President for help and get much needed reform going. The America Bar Association filed a report to the House of Delegates on the Death Penalty Due Process Review Project on execution of any individual who was 21 years old or younger at the time of the offense. I cited a few statistics and language out of the report.

Now, I'll state it again, as I stated before: who's going to save us! We need federal legislation on juvenile and young adolescent reform. Too many of us were to have allegedly to commit crimes in our youth, and received life without parole sentences. Crimes committed when our brains were still developing and we were vulnerable to follow others and subject to peer pressure to commit violent acts. In turn, with no federal laws protecting the juveniles and young adolescents, the federal courts still have the ability to give us numerous life sentences then throw us in the dangerous United States Penitentiaries to be raised by the two-tiered system that is in place for black and brown people. A system with no hope of relief for people like me with over 50 programs which equates to over a thousand hours of prison programming, obtained a GED, mentoring and tutoring other inmates keeping constant employment in or around the education department, self-taught jailhouse lawyer who has helped countless inmates with their legal problems and I haven't been in trouble in 10 years and I only have one incident report after 17 years in maximum security prisons. What more do we have to do or prove that we're reformed, if given the chance by the federal legislators to prove it. We need reform.

As a Reformed Juvenile Lifer, and self-taught jailhouse lawyer with close to 17 years of being incarcerated, I understand how hard it is to get any type of legislation passed in Washington. But, the juvenile and young adolescent issue should be a priority and considered a "public health crisis" or maybe a "human rights crisis" against black and brown people. Or maybe a violation of the Eighth Amendment, as stated in the Supreme Court decision of Miller v. Alabama(2012) but draws a line at 18 years old. So, if the Supreme Court doesn't save us then who's going to save us? Is it the federal legislators? Is it President Trump? If not, then how can we say as Americans that we won't let the youth smoke cigarettes but we'll send them to do life in prison, even though our distinguished professors and experts like Dr. Laurence Steinberg says that "the science would certainly say there's significant brain maturation that continues to go on at least until age 21, if not beyond."

We need reform and help in this matter. Who's going to save us?

After finishing the piece, I went and made 100 copies. I sent this article to every major and small newspaper companies, a few magazines, professors, advocates, and Washington lawmakers. Nobody responded to the article. It wasn't surprising that nobody responded because that's the norm when your considered a violent racketeering drug trafficker, and not a young offender that made a grave mistake. The Powers that Be shut you out of society - everything, and the regular folks don't bother to pay attention to what's going on until its to late. Only when they're charged with a Federal offense, and realize how grave and ambiguous the laws can be. It's only at this moment when they start begging for help, and seeing how hard it is to get any type of relief from the Courts. How hard it is to get anybody to advocate for you. How hard it is to be incarcerated in federal prison. Especially, with a life without parole sentence.

These pictures were taking during our pre-trial at FDC Philly. My co-defendants, Vincent and Jamain, along with Hussein and Saleem.

CHAPTER 4

Are You A Racketeer

For 19 years, I studied the Federal laws concerning RICO and VICAR. And, for a number of years I was so confused and frustrated with these two separate federal offenses. I'm not alone with this confusion. Lawyers, Prosecutors, and federal Judges also get the two offenses confused. Take a look at a case from out of the Southern District of West Virginia's Charleston Division, in the case of David Keith Barbeito. In Barbeito, a federal district court had to weed through these confusing offenses. The federal court went on to state that, "care must be taken, however, to take account the differences in the statute so as to avoid confusing elements. VICAR's requirement of proof of an enterprise engaged in racketeering activity is one such element that must be distinguished from RICO'S pattern-of racketeering element because the parties have at times confused these elements throughout the course of this case.

"VICAR contains a definition for the term "enterprise" and shares its definition of racketeering activity" with RICO. It defines as "enterprise" as "any partnership, corporation, association, or other legal entity, and any union or group of individuals associated in fact although not a legal entity, which is engaged in, or the activities of which affect, interstate or foreign commerce." 18 USC §1959(b)(2). This is identical to RICO' definition of "enterprise" with one minor exception: the RICO enterprise definition does not include the interstate commerce nexus language.

“"Racketeering activity" in VICAR is given the same meaning as the definition of the term for RICO. §1959(b)(1). "Racketeering activity" is defined as, "(A) any act or threat involving murder, kidnapping, gambling, arson, robbery, bribery, extortion, dealing in obscene matter, or dealing in a controlled substance or listed chemical..., which is chargeable under State law and punishable by imprisonment for more than one year; (B) any act which is indictable under any of the following provisions of [the United States Code]." 18 USC §1961(1).

"Unlike RICO, the word "pattern" does not appear in VICAR. Whereas RICO requires proof that the accused engaged in a "pattern of racketeering activity", VICAR requires proof of an "enterprise engaged in racketeering activity" -- without reference to a pattern. There is no statutory definition for the phrase "engaged in racketeering activity", nor is there clear guidance."

What! Congress did not explain no terms under these statutes. Not even what "murder" was defined to mean. This is so confusing because a young offender can be convicted under the RICO/VICAR statutes for committing any degree of murder along with the slightest connection with any group or gang or associate-in-fact from the neighborhood. A young offender can receive the maximum sentence of incarceration -life without parole, if convicted under VICAR alone for any degree of murder then receive a mandatory life without parole sentence.

Now, this all should make a sane person sit back and think that - if these highly intelligent Lawyers, Prosecutors and Judges can not grasp the definition and terms of what RICO and VICAR demand for a conviction then how could a young offender. How can a juvenile/young offender comprehend these things? Especially, with all the childhood trauma, undeveloped brains, and constant peer-pressure clouding their thoughts; how could they come up with the formation of a sophisticated drug trafficking conspiracy/RICO enterprise? It's impossible, if you asked the professors and experts in this field of study who authored these reports. But, the Government and Courts are silent on the matter, and thinks differently on this issue.

We know that they may think differently on the nature of a young offender forming and participating in a RICO enterprise because the meanings are not defined. Anybody can be labeled a racketeer - you or young offenders.

Since, I'm a member of this injustice I have been laser focused on proving how outlandish these two offenses are. Believe me, the road has been extremely hard. A few years back, I was invited to enter a writing contest for an upcoming book named, "What We Know". The Center for America Progress, and the Formerly Incarcerated Convicted Peoples and Family movement along with the New Press were creating this book. The group were looking for stories on specific, serious, well-defined suggestion for how to improve a particular aspect of any part of our current system. The top 12-20 essays would be published in the finished book, and the authors would receive $500 each. Authors of the top 50 essays that were not selected for publication would also receive $50 each. I was a runner-up in this contest. I received a copy of the book but not the money.

The essay that I submitted was named, "Are You A Racketeer?" Here's the full essay:

ARE YOU A RACKETEER?

Well that depends on if the Government wants you to be a racketeer or not. The term was coined by the Government to mean -someone who engages in racketeering; specifically - someone who earns money from organized crime. And, racketeering was also defined as a system of organized crime traditionally involving the extortion of money from businesses by intimidation, violence or other illegal methods. A pattern of illegal activity carried out as part of an enterprise that is owned or controlled by those engaged in the illegal activity.

At first glance, this meaning is fairly straight forward as to its literal application towards organized criminal activity. A criminal that belongs to an organized business. Right? Just imagine when you were a kid playing with all the other kids in your neighborhood. Playing basketball, football and all the other fun activities that kids do and bond over. Then, fast-forward to becoming great friends with these same kids from the neighborhood going in to your teenager and, or young adults years. And, through out these teenaged or young adults years a few of them may have veered a little to the left and started committing some minor drug crimes. Some of you may even had committed a violent crime - for whatever reasons. Crimes that were isolated and having nothing to do with you or any other group of people. All the crimes may have just been committed in the same neighborhood. Could you image one day of being labeled a racketeer or gang member because of some particular neighborhood, street or group of individuals that you know of or come from? The answer would be no for most. Well, think again because it could be done if the Government wishes or desires for you to fit in this or that particular category of individuals. I'm a prime example of how the Government can come in an urban neighborhood and snatch a group of people off of the street. Once off of the streets then federally indicted in a whole array of federal offenses. My case arose from a State and Federal investigation of drug trafficking and murder in a small neighborhood in Chester, Pennsylvania known as the Highland Gardens. Where, large numbers of disaffected and impoverished youth, having been utterly failed by the school and public health systems of the community sold drugs openly. Among these youth were me and several others. I was indicted in February of 2003 at the age of 23 years old. The indictment stated that I was part of a violent cocaine RICO/VICAR enterprise which started in or around the years of 1996 and lasted all the way until December of 2002. I was 16 years old at the start of this, alleged, RICO and drug

- cocaine enterprise and so were most of my co-defendants. I was born on June 24, 1979. Nobody was over the age of 17 years old when the alleged enterprise was supposed to be thought of and formed. The theory at trial was that we came up with an idea to form the enterprise as teenagers. The evidence adduced at trial indicated that me and several others intersected and intertwined our personal relationships together and formed an association or drug enterprise who murdered in furtherance of the enterprise. In addition, the Government argued at trial and presented testimony that the initial agreement to murder 'people' occurred at the age of 16 years old. At the time when also the initial agreement to form the enterprise occurred.

While the majority of us were youth, as the indictment and evidence at trial stated but this group or enterprise was anything less than organized and together. Unfortunately though, the manner in which I was indicted and tried made my convictions a pre-ordained conclusion. Charges that were not related were joined, we were tried to a death-qualified, and anonymous jury and all manner of irrelevances were permitted under the guise of co-conspirator statements and evidence of conspiracy. To make a long story short, I went to the penalty phase of my death-qualified trial and the jury came back with a 11 to 1 vote for death. I'm not on death row because the lawyers explained that we were teenagers who grew up in a violent city and environment. I was sent to spend the rest of my life in maximum-security prisons because the Government had the authority to label this group of teenagers racketeers who formed an illegal enterprise.

In addition to being able to indict such a large group of teenagers and, or young adults based on the enterprise theory, the Government was able to bring another far-reaching and ambiguous offense to the fore-front - Violent Crimes In Aid Racketeering(VICAR), 18 USC §1959(a). VICAR is another vicious weapon that goes hand in hand with the enterprise theory. VICAR is the federal offense that I was charged with, in connection to the alleged murder claims. The average citizen couldn't even image where to begin when trying to defend themselves from such charges. Federal offenses that are not clearly defined, totally ambiguous in nature but yet enforced thoroughly by the Government to pursue any one they deem fit.

In 2009, the Supreme Court aided the Government's efforts to snatch groups of teenagers and, or young adults off the street under the guise of participating in a VICAR enterprise by deciding a case called Boyle v. United States(2009). In this particular case, Boyle was charged in connection with a series of bank thefts that were allegedly conducted by a group that was loosely organized and did not appear to have had a leader or hierarchy. The trial court refused to give Boyle's proposed instruction that the government was required to prove that the RICO enterprise had an ascertainable structural hierarchy distinct from the charged predicated acts. The trial court instead instructed the jury that an association of individuals without structural hierarchy could form an enterprise. The Supreme Court held that an association-in-fact enterprise had to have a "structure". However, the instructions did not have to include the term "structure", and the jury was correctly and adequately instructed. The enumerated enterprises under 18 USC §1961(4) broadly encompassed any group of individuals associated-in-fact and were not limited to "business-like entities." However, additional structural features such as hierarchy or a chain of command were not required. Boyle went on to argue that he was not apart of any RICO enterprise because the group had no leader, rules or business like structure. Boyle was right if the Court looked at the common sense understanding of the word business. An association-in-fact enterprise, as the term is used in RICO/VICAR statutes, need not have any decision making process and may be made on an ad hoc basis and by any number of methods... Members of the group need not have fixed roles... The group need not have a name, regular meetings, dues, established rules and regulations, disciplinary procedure, or induction or initiation ceremonies. What type of business or matter of fact what type of illegal business or gang doesn't require any of these stipulations? But, the Supreme Court then went on to confuse the ruling even more stating that, 'the enterprise must have at least three structural features: a person, relationship, and longevity sufficient to permit these associates to pursue the enterprise purpose. What? I don't understand how so. This is exactly the reaction that any average American teenager or young adult would say or should say. How could the Government have it both ways? Is this really the true meaning of an enterprise or is the Court aiding and abetting the Government's unconstitutional actions?

The Supreme Court did a great injustice to the American people with this ruling. Now, who are we supposed to depend on to strike down such an ambiguous understanding of this enterprise concept, as it pertains to an alleged racketeer? The Court handed the Government a vicious weapon to use in order to go in to any community in America and indict any and, or all that ever lived there on RICO enterprise charges. This could be 8 people, as we were, or 60 people it doesn't matter. The number of people doesn't matter because of such an expanded definition of the enterprise term.

There were a few issues left out in the Boyle decision though. The Supreme Court only had an opportunity to define what an association-in-fact enterprise meant. The Court never had a chance to address the broader scope of the Violent Crimes In Aid of Racketeering, 18 USC §1959(a), offense. Which is also mind blowing in and of itself.

Title 18, Section 1959 provides for punishment of any individual who "murders, kidnaps, maims, assaults with a dangerous weapon, commits assault resulting in serious bodily injury upon, or threatens to commit a crime of violence against any individual in violation of the laws of any State or the United States, or attempts or conspires so to do" for the purpose of entering, maintaining or increasing his position in a criminal enterprise. Thus, to establish a VICAR offense the following five elements must be established beyond a reasonable doubt:

1. *that the organization is a RICO enterprise:*
2. *that the enterprise was engaged in racketeering activity as defined in RICO;*
3. *that the defendant had a position in the enterprise;*
4. *that the defendant committed the alleged crime of violence in violation of federal or state law; and*
5. *that the defendant's general purpose in so doing was to maintain or increase his position in the enterprise.*

Once again you can see the Government's vicious weapon is grounded deeply in this statute - RICO/VICAR enterprise.

So, we know from the very beginning how far this particular offense's reach goes. But, for the sake of brevity let's just deal with the mens rea element of VICAR. A particular persons intention to commit the violent crime, as it pertains to this statute. As stated before, a VICAR conviction requires proof that a defendant act "for the purpose of gaining entrance to or maintaining or increasing position in an enterprise." The phrase "maintaining or increasing position in an enterprise" is not defined in the statute. Surprising! Congress did not articulate how this element was suppose to operate but several district courts around the Country has tried to attempt to. Although lacking tremendously, district courts have once again enforced an ambiguous element in to a catch-all provision for people allegedly apart of an enterprise.

One meaning has been clarified by a number of cases that define what it means to "maintain" or "increase" one's position in an enterprise. It goes on to state an example that, Racketeer A's conduct satisfies this motive element of VICAR if ----

** committing the violent crime was an "integral aspect of membership"*

** if the conduct was expected by virtue of the defendant's membership in the enterprise*

** if the racketeer role is that of an "enforcer" satisfies the motive element if he murders a person who has attacked a leader of the enterprise, if failing to retaliate would undermine his role as an enforcer*

** the element is satisfied if there is a perceived threat to the enterprise and failure to the respond to the threat with violence would undermine the defendant's position in the organization*

** violent crimes committed to protect the enterprise's racketeering activities also generally satisfy the motive element*

** an enterprise's expectations of its members maybe relevant, at least as circumstantial evidence that a defendant acted with the purpose of maintaining or increasing his position in the enterprise*

** violent acts committed to aid the enterprise by cultivating its reputation for violence can satisfy the motive element if the defendant's actions in support of this end maintained his position in the enterprise*

** the racketeering enterprise purpose does not have to be a "general purpose"*

Is there anyway to escape this catch-all provision? This is just the mens rea of VICAR, and not the other four elements that a person would have to defend themselves against.

VICAR's motive element can be demonstrated in a variety of ways, often by mere inferences from the facts. How could this be legal? How would a reasonable defense be mounted against the enterprise theory, and just for starters the motive element of "maintaining" or increasing your position in a "RICO enterprise" when you have eight different ways you have to defend against one element? This has 5th and 6th Amendment constitutional violations written all over it. This specific issue of applying ambiguous laws to unsuspecting teenagers and, or young adults is wrong.

What I would suggest is that an effort be made and geared to informing more people about the ambiguous written federal laws. Laws that could get any individuals or legitimate organizations in a tight and uncomfortable situation that they may or may not be able to get out of. Take for example the National Organization For Women, Inc. This organization was charged and convicted for conspiracy to shut down abortion clinics because they were labeled a racketeering enterprise. This Women's organization went all the way to the Supreme Court which once again sided with the Government.

We, as a people living in America need to open our eyes up. This needs to end. There is hope, and change can be done if serious efforts in order to move forward with creative ways to correct this unjust actions of the Courts and Government. Like, first, there should be an effort to change the model of these criminal justice reform movements. The movements should be formed and operated like a business. The 'Business of Social Justice'. It should be ran how a presidential campaign is ran and funded. With an emphasis on educating the public about the horrors of the criminal justice system and how its still being ran like slavery. But, a substantial amount of effort and money is going to be needed.

Generating the money to change public opinions can be done. This could be done through social media, entertainers donating their time and money, and other funding avenues through corporate companies who believe in the mission of social justice. I mean really believing in our mission and not there for publicity or trying to give in order to have the leaders of the mission change the agenda in the middle of the fight.

Money is needed, and no serious change can be done without it because the other sides war chest is hefty and unlimited with cash, high-priced and experienced lawyers, and we can not forget about the inherited judicial prejudice against certain people of color.

We need to hire the best lobbyist firms, get advertising spots on all the major cable and news networks as well as the major newspapers in the Country. Frame the business model just like the presidential campaigns are formed and ran. I do not see it no other way. The next step in this crusade would be attempting to get the young and savvy millenniums on board. This is key. They're the future lawyers, judges, lawmakers, jurors and voting block. In addition to these career paths and obligations as citizens, the millenniums are the ones who are making a different in all spheres of life. Take for instance the Parkland survivors. This group of young adults had the policy makers, literally, scared of losing their various congressional seats in the State and Federal governments. These young adults had them feeling uncertain and uncomfortable with sticking to their old-fashioned prejudice ways.

We could use that same type of pressure the Parkland survivors used so that the next phase could be carried out. The forming of committees to guard against the ambiguous and unconstitutional laws being created. Communities that have regular, but well-informed, citizens who view and participate in the drafting of laws. The old ways are not working or it may be to seeped in pre-conceived prejudices and special interest groups who's concerns are not of the people. Either way, We The People must have a bigger say or role in the law making process. Our elected officials are dropping the ball, not abiding by the Constitutional principles, and not heeding our cries for justice and fairness for all.

Maybe these new suggestions, taken as a whole, could help or maybe not. We'll never know until somebody makes the first step or attempt to change the model of criminal justice and, or social justice reform and treat it like an entrepreneur would when trying to market a new product to the world and having the Government frame their laws and policy around the product - us. If this is unachievable or to outlandish of an ideal to accomplish then you may just be the next person who the Government labels a racketeer with ties to a loosely and informally organized group.

My main focus on the essay was to show the fact that, young offenders and anybody else who is involved in drug dealing and violent crimes could find themselves indicted federally. And, this is exactly what the skeptics have criticized in the past that so-called Urban Street gangs are often said to be young and impressionable and street gangs are arguably less organized than the Mafia. This was noticed back in the early 90's.

Basically, what I am saying is "Stay Woke". They have been filling these federal prisons up with kids - young offenders, for several decades, and nobody is trying to advocate or bring any attention to these racketeering laws that's targeting young offenders. These young offenders who have been in prison for decades, and growing old and grey because they will never be released.

Homes in the Highland Gardens neighborhood to date.

CHAPTER 5

Imperfect People

America has a history of being cruel to us. Especially, the people who govern the Country. They govern us by a document. A document that was fought over, thought of, argued over, and signed while Black Americans were still enslaved. A Federal Court of Appeals Judge once described this piece of paper that governs the United States of America like this, "it is a document designed to govern **imperfect people,** the Constitution does not demand perfect trials and errors do not necessarily require reversal of a conviction. More than thirty years ago, the Supreme Court reminded us: "As we have stressed on more than one occasion, the Constitution entitles a criminal defendant to a fair trial, not a perfect one." This statement is so true, as stated by a Government institution that once viewed all Black Americans as one fifth of a man. But, what the Judge, and the Highest Court failed to mention were the deeply rooted systemic racism inside the criminal justice system.

Many criminal justice advocates and, or reformers are trying to expose the flaws of this wicked designed system. They're fighting for justice reform on many fronts, but most of the widely publicized fights surround non-violent drug offenders, crack-to-cocaine disparity, bail reform and other issues. Very few, and I mean a very small minority of advocates are bringing forth an argument for young offenders. Not only young offenders but "once" violent young offenders that have been rotting in maximum-security prisons for decades. Let's take a look at Joe Ligon long journey of incarceration to eventual freedom.

Joe Ligon was incarcerated in February of 1953 at the age of 15 years old, given a mandatory life sentence after pleading not-guilty to charges stemming from a robbery and stabbing spree in Philadelphia with four other teenage boys which resulted in two people fatally being killed. He spent 68 years in prison for some violent crimes that he allegedly committed as a juvenile. Whether he did it or not, this was a foolish and grave juvenile mistake that cost this man 68 years of incarceration. It took one person to actually step-up, that cared, in order for Joe Ligon to gain his freedom for a conviction that stemmed from juvenile conduct. We need more lawyers like Bradley Bridge, a lawyer from Philadelphia. But, what I am trying to high-light is federal inmates who were teenagers when they were accused of forming or participating in drug conspiracies. These young offenders who were charged with federal drug trafficking conspiracies, forming racketeering enterprises, committing violent crimes in aid of racketeering and participating in Continuing Criminal Enterprises that spans from their early teenage years in to their mid-twenties. It is a shame. A growing body of research on adolescent development confirms that teenagers are indeed inherently different from adults, not only in their behaviors but also (and of course relatedly) in the ways their brain function. In addition, it is also a proven fact that childhood trauma turns into teen violence. Almost 100% of violent offenders have early trauma. The trauma changes a teens brain architecture. For example, witnessing or being a victim of neighborhood violence, living with people that have drug and alcohol problems, family members involved in drug dealing and violent acts, enduring extreme economic hardship/poverty, and all the other experiences that corresponds with riskier behavior and establishes that there's a greater likelihood of a kid involvement in the criminal legal system.

At least since the early 1900's, the justice system in the United States has recognized that juvenile (young) offenders are not the same as adults and has tried to incorporate those differences into law and policy. The law and policy had once been favorable to juvenile/young offenders in the beginning. In 1941, the "Committee on Punishment for Crime of the Judicial Conference of Senior Circuit Judges" drafted a proposal giving special consideration to young offenders and submitted the proposal to Congress. This proposed legislation was the precursor of the Federal Youth Corrections Act ("FYCA") - 18 USC §5002 et seq. (1976). In 1950, the FYCA was passed to provide guidance to the federal judges when sentencing a "young offender" under the age of 22, and a "young adult offender" between the ages of 22 and 26, that included segregation from adult offenders in prison and alternatives to imprisonment, such as rehabilitation and treatment.

The FYCA was designed to: make available for discretionary use of the Federal Judges a system for the sentencing and treatment of persons under 22 years of age who have been convicted of crime in the United States Courts that will promote the rehabilitation of those who in the opinion of the sentencing judges show promise of becoming useful citizens, and so, will avoid the degenerative and needless transformation of these young persons in to habitual criminals. The FYCA had strong rehabilitative purposes. However, a sentence may be given to a defendant who is over 22 and not yet 26 Years of age at the time of conviction, if the sentencing court affirmatively finds that there are reasonable grounds to believe that the defendant will benefit from treatment provided under the Federal Youth Corrections Act. 18 USC §4216.

All of these special requirements and focus on young offenders were formed on a common sense basis. There were studies but no sophisticated studies or research, policy debates or any of the distractions that formed these federal legislatures decisions to pass the laws. The Federal Judges just asked for discretion to help these young offenders. We need more strong-willed Judges to step up and demand this now. For much of American history a central rationale of sentencing has been the rehabilitation or "reformation" of the defendant.

In 1984, Congress changed its focus from youth offenders being rehabilitated to the "war on drugs". Congress came down hard on young black and brown citizens of America. The Federal Government targeted the inner-cities of America where clusters of Black and Brown young people lived and hung out.

Congress passed the Sentencing Reform Act, which "channeled judges' discretion by establishing a framework to govern their consideration and imposition of sentence." In relevant part, the Act provided:

The court, in determining whether to impose a term of imprisonment, and if a term of imprisonment is to be imposed, in determining the length of the term, shall consider the factors set forth in [18 USC] section 3553(a) to the extent that they are applicable, recognizing that imprisonment is not an appropriate means of promoting correction and rehabilitation.

18 USC §3582(a).

The Supreme Court explains, this provision later on, that lawmakers doubts "that prison programs could 'rehabilitate individuals on a routine basis' - or that parole officers could 'determine accurately whether or when a particular prisoner ha[d] been rehabilitated."" This decision adopted by the lawmakers abandoned "all" hope for a majority of the young offenders incarcerated in the federal system. In 1990, President George H.W. Bush launched the "Decade of the Brain" initiative to "enhance public awareness of benefits to be derived from brain research." With this investment by President Bush, advances in neuroimaging techniques now allow researchers to evaluate a living human brain. It took almost forty years for any federal entity to step up to these harsh stances by Congress and move the law forward.

The Supreme Court took a turn, for a chance, then followed the science. Social Scientists and Neuroscientists along with other experts recognize that the development of the human brain, and the inhibitions that go along with it, are not complete until well into the 20's. Austin Sarat, an Amherst law professor noted that, "No child should be sentenced to life in prison without parole even if they commit horrendous crimes. Why? Because, as former Supreme Court Justice Anthony Kennedy once noted, "any parents know" children are different from adults. They lack the judgment and self-control that come with adulthood. Absent these qualities, imposing severe punishment is unjust and inappropriate. As Kennedy rightly observed, a "lack of maturity and an underdeveloped sense of responsibility are found in youth more often than adults and are more understandable among the young. These qualities often result in impetuous and ill-considered actions and decisions."

The Supreme Court took a stance, but no statutory federal law has been reached to account for this newly recognized brain science, as it relates to young offenders who committed the crimes below their mid-twenties.

Although, in 2017, the United States Sentencing Commission produced its first report on "Youthful Offenders." The Commission presented information about youthful offenders, who for the purposes of that report were defined as persons age 25 or younger at the time they were sentenced in the Federal system. The study acknowledged that youthful offenders account for about 18 percent of all federal offenders sentenced between fiscal years 2010 and 2015. This study was conducted because little current information had been published on the issue. The Commission explained that brains continue to develop until approximately age twenty-five, and that developmental differences relevant to sentencing generally persist until around that age. This is a great sign, but this report does nothing to help the young offenders who were teenagers when the initial conspiracy or RICO enterprise started. It doesn't help against mandatory-minimum sentences of life without parole either. The Commission's report targets a certain period of youthful offenders from 2015, and that were sentenced under 25 years old. This is a big difference from what I am speaking out about. But, despite the difference the Commission reports that, "96 received life imprisonment sentences when sentenced for their federal conviction. Five of these offenders were younger than 20 at the time of sentencing." The report went further to state, "29 received life sentences for firearm offense, 25 for extortion and/or racketeering, 17 for drug trafficking, ten for murder, three for auto-theft, and two for kidnapping."

Now, this is just for the years between 2010-2015. This doesn't include the thousands of young offenders that committed "crimes" under the age of 25 years old - not sentenced under 25 years old who's serving "mandatory" life without parole sentences. The young offenders who's not being properly recognized. All they're asking for from the lawmakers, and Federal Courts is to **follow the science,** as the saying goes, then create some sound Federal legislation.

Books that I wrote while in Federal prison.

"Society changes, knowledge accumulates, we learn, sometimes from our mistakes, punishments that did not seem cruel and unusual at one time, may, in light of reason and experience, be found cruel and unusual later."

JUSTICE KENNEDY NOTED IN GRAHAM V. FLORIDA (2011)

CHAPTER 6

Ratification

A lot of people that don't have any dealings with the Federal legal system could never image that kids could be held liable for a drug conspiracy, or a RICO enterprise that conduct relates to a variety of crimes. Well, Donnell Williams was 11 years old when he began participating in the illegal activities of the R Street crew, which was later named or labeled a Sophisticated Urban Street Gang - a racketeering enterprise. A corner and crew from Washington, D.C. that just so happened to be the first time that a RICO charge were brought against young offenders in the District of Columbia. There were two other so-called sophisticated urban street gangs around the Country that got hit with this Federal offense -RICO. There is the one group out of New York City called the "Westies" and another involving a Chicago gang named the "El Rukns".

Studies have tried to enforce this theory that urban street gangs were the problem. The theory was surrounded around the crack-cocaine trade, as the primary example for transforming many fraternal, juvenile organizations into highly sophisticated organized crime entities. One law review by Lesly Suzanne Bonney stated that, urban street gangs have accrued much of the same economic and political power traditionally associated with more sophisticated organized crime entities, such as the Mafia. Ms. Bonney went on to argue that, "virtually every urban area within the United States houses sophisticated street gangs; moreover, gangs no longer limit themselves to traditional urban settings. As gangs become more prevalent in society, they become harder to identify as criminal organizations. Thus, while sophisticated streets gangs are often successful in infiltrating legitimate businesses, they continue to walk a fine line between criminal and legal activities." This is a clear bias view of teenagers selling drugs in the neighborhood. Donnell Williams turned eighteen on December 18, 1989, and nineteen when he was indicted for his involvement in the conspiracy and for various related substantive offenses. He was convicted of RICO conspiracy, narcotics conspiracy, unlawful distribution of narcotics, and unlawful use of a communications facility.

Donnell received a life without parole sentence for these crimes.

For anybody to understand how this can happen needs to be explained a little further on how these ambiguous laws are structured. Most, so-called sophisticated urban street gangs sell drugs on a regular basis. At least this is what the reports state. But, some urban street gangs, as stated by the reports, have reached the level of "major crime and terrorist organizations" engaging in racketeering activity other than narcotics distribution, robbery, extortion, bribery, kidnapping, and obstruction of justice.

For the simple reason that, these crimes can be committed and exist spurred the Federal Government to focus its scrutiny on so-called sophisticated urban street gangs.

Let's look a bit closer in to these specific federal offenses. Conspiracy is a law Congress first enacted in 1909, as the Conspiracy Act (offenses against the United States); which prosecutors used to convict mobsters and other criminals without any physical, corroborating or scientific evidence. In 1925, Judge Learned Hand referred to conspiracy as "that darling of the modern prosecutor's nursey." Twenty-four years later, Justice Jackson, in a memorable opinion, referred to the history of conspiracy as "exemplifying the tendency of a principle to expand itself to the limit of its logic." The Justice went on to describe the crime of conspiracy, as, so vague that it almost defines definition. Despite certain elementary and essential elements, it also, chameleon-like, takes on a special coloration from each of the many independent offenses on which it may be overlaid. It is always "predominately mental in composition" because it consists primarily of a meeting of minds and an intent. The crime come down to, us, wrapped in vague but unpleasant connotations."

In 1948, Congress enacted Title 18 of the United States Code, Section, "Conspiracy to Commit Offense or to Defraud the United States"; then in 1970, added Title 21 USC, Section 846, "Attempt and Conspiracy" to their arsenal to prosecute drug offenses and allow prosecutors to seek the same sentence as provided for the primary offense; e.g., life without parole for certain drug offenses. When, Congress enacted the Comprehensive Drug Abuse Prevention and Control Act, which separated drugs into five "schedules" according to their potential for abuse. The statute assigned penalties in accordance with a drug's schedule and whether it was a narcotic, without considering quantity. That changed in 1984, when Congress introduced quantities to the statute. Controlled Substances Penalties Amendments Act of 1984 (codified at 21 USC §841(b)).

But, two years later, Congress enacted another draconian law. A law that federal defendants, and advocates are still fighting over 40 years later. The Anti-Drug Abuse Act introduced mandatory-minimums for offenses involving specified weights of particular drugs. This is where the disparity between crack-cocaine and powder cocaine originated. A lot of federal inmates received life sentences because of this drug statute and disparity issue.

With these laws in mind, and attached to a drug conspiracy, - a criminal conspiracy may be based on little more than informants, cooperating co-defendants that sometimes who benefit from the Government with a reduced sentence or immediate dismissal of charges; and witnesses claiming a person planned to or committed a crime. Under Section 371, if the government convinces the judge or jurors of an overt act used to activate the plan to violate the law, normally a person gets convicted then goes to federal prison. The maximum penalty for this crime is five years of imprisonment and, or fine. The Government does not have to prove an overt act was committed under Section 846. Overt acts may be as simple as making a phone call or instructing someone who to see or where to go to buy illicit drugs, weapons, murder or anything used to knowingly violate federal laws.

Another weapon used by the Government on young offenders is a federal statute named - Violent Crimes in Aid of Racketeering, 18 USC §1959(a), as I expounded on this statute earlier. The history behind this statute is clear. Congress designed VICAR to supplement the racketeering offense, and hence VICAR may be used in addition to the RICO offense. The reasons for this is because of what the Federal Senate Report on VICAR had found. The report stated that, "with respect to [section 1959], the Committee concluded that the need for Federal jurisdiction is clear, in view of the Federal Government's strong interest, as recognized in existing statutes, in suppressing the activities of organized criminal enterprises, and the fact that the FBI's experience and network of informants and intelligence with respect to such enterprises will often facilitate a successful federal investigation where local authorities might be stymied. Here again, however, the Committee does not intend that all such offenses should be prosecuted federally. Murder, kidnapping, and assault also violate State law and the States will still have an important role to play in many such cases that are committed as an integral part of an organized crime operation." In addition to this report, Federal Courts around the Country has decided that there were substantial similarities between RICO and VICAR enterprises. Basically, the body of law under RICO regarding "enterprises" were to be used in VICAR prosecutions.

VICAR is such a vague Federal offense. The Government could, literally, piece together a VICAR trial, if they wanted to target a certain group of individuals that grew-up together, in an urban neighborhood, and hung together from time-to-time, or knew each other simply from the neighborhood. Any level of culpability, intent and circumstances around drug dealing and violent crimes could land a young offender on a VICAR or RICO case. These two federal offenses weren't supposed to be applied to poverty-stricken kids, juveniles, or young offenders but that's certainly how the Government has been utilizing these judicial weapons for decades without any lawmakers stopping it. No advocates have complained or came to the young offenders defense either.

With such a weapon being used by the Government nobody has a chance. Especially, young offenders that enter in to such drug conspiracies or RICO enterprises.

As you can see from the Senate Report, these draconian and vague laws were for highly organized criminal enterprises or drug trafficking organizations. Criminals that formed these drug conspiracies or RICO enterprises when they were adults who knew what type of illicit activity that they were getting themselves involved in. Not for young offenders who were just dealing drugs or committing local violent crimes without any sense of the consequences that followed.

But this whole issue comes down to young offenders forming or entering a conspiracy/ enterprise in their teenage years. And being able to receive some relief from those draconian sentences boils down to one legal term - ratification.

Ratification is a noun that stems from the word ratify. Such a term means 'to adopt or affirm (as the prior act or contract of an agent) by express or implied consent with the effect of original authorization [unable to rescind the contract because he ratified it by accepting the benefits]. The concept has been similar to the contract "ratification" doctrine: just as a minor legally incapable of entering a contract may nonetheless be found to have "ratified" a contract by taking actions after attaining majority consistent with an intent to be bound by it. So, the law, as it stands today is that; a young offender may ratify his pre-eighteen participation in a conspiracy by continued participation after attaining the age of 18 years old. By this standard, it is well established through case law that federal courts have jurisdiction over conspiracies begun while a person was a minor but completed after his eighteen birthday because a conspiracy/enterprise is a continuing crime that endures until its objectives are either completed or abandoned. Although, the crime of conspiring to act is completed. Interesting type of legal concept right, or more like a bunch of confusing theories for any young offender to understand. Yet, if racketeering and conspiracies are continuing offenses with its original objectives made in your youth -- why then all the evidence of "child trauma", "lack of undeveloped brain function", "lack of maturity" and "no sense of responsibility" cannot be taking into consideration to negate elements of the offense or guilt? The Federal District Courts are split on whether or not a court must instruct the jury to disregard evidence of pre-eighteen conduct assessing guilt. My jury was never instructed to disregard any conduct or evidence from the ages of 16-18. This didn't occur for any person in my case. One of the lawyers, in the case, tried to get this pre-eighteen conduct struck from the evidence and from going to the jury. The Judge denied this request then threaten sanctions because the Judge felt it was a frivolous argument. Although, the lawyers had several Supreme Court and other Circuit Court opinions supporting the request for relief.

It doesn't make sense for the Government to be able to use the ratification doctrine to get a person indicted, convicted and sentenced on all of your pre-eighteen conduct but you can't use this same evidence, in order to apply for the protections articulated in the Supreme Court cases. Not only that, a person can not use the new scholarly reports, towards the initial agreements of the drug trafficking offense and RICO enterprise to support the fact that you were a young offender at the time of the offense.

All of the agreements to take part in a drug conspiracy, to form or take part in a racketeering enterprise, and to commit violent acts were testified to have occurred when everybody were teenagers in my case. But, none of us can benefit from the Supreme Court decisions that deals with juvenile/young offenders. Congress needs to address this issue because juvenile/young offenders don't have a clue about the circumstances and consequences of a drug conspiracy, racketeering crimes or VICAR offenses. Age must be considered, as an element of the offense for a drug conspiracy, racketeering and VICAR enterprises. The gold standard for any juvenile/young offender to receive an unusually long sentence, or the maximum allowed penalty of life without parole.

My profile picture on change.org

"A people confident in its laws and institutions should not be ashamed of mercy. The greatest of poets reminds us that mercy is "mightiest in the mightiest. It becomes the throned monarch better than his crown." I hope more lawyers involved in the pardon process will say to Chief Executives, "Mr. President," or "Your Excellency, the

Governor, this young man has not served his full sentence, but he has served long enough. Give him what only you can give him. Give him another chance. Give him a priceless gift. Give him Liberty." For "still, the prisoner is a person; still he or she is part of the family of humankind."

- Justice Kennedy, American Bar Association speech in 2003

CHAPTER 7

New Criminal Law Reform

There is slight, and I mean very slim hope on the horizon despite Congress' lack of interest in directly protecting juveniles/young offenders from receiving a life sentence. On December 21, 2018, Congress passed the First Step Act. For decades, the Bureau of Prisons had unlimited and unreviewable discretion to block the sentencing judge from considering a motion to reduce an inmate's sentence, even where "extraordinary and compelling reasons" warrant such a reduction. 18 USC §3582 (c)(1)(A). Until the First Step Act, if the Bureau of Prisons denied a request for compassionate release, an inmate had no ability to ask the court for help or "compassion" when the circumstances that presented themselves indicated that a reduction in sentence was the only decent and compassionate option. In 2018, Congress changed the law toward a more inmate-friendly one. The compassionate release law, pursuant to 18 USC §3582(c)(1)(A) provides:

> (c) Modification of an Imposed Term of Imprisonment - The Court may not modify a term of imprisonment once it has been imposed except that -(1) in any case -
>
> (A) the Court, upon motion of the Director of the Bureau of Prisons or upon motion of the Defendant after the defendant has fully exhausted all administrative rights to appeal a failure to the Bureau of Prisons to bring a motion on the defendant's behalf or the lapse of 30 days from the receipt of such a request by the Warden of the defendant's facility, whichever is earlier, may reduce the term of imprisonment (and may impose a term of probation or supervised release with or without conditions that does not exceed the unserved portion of the original term of imprisonment), after considering the factors set forth in section 3553(a) to the extent that --
>
> (i) extraordinary and compelling reasons warrant such a reduction...
>
> And that such a reduction is consistent with the applicable policy statements issued by the Sentencing Commission... Furthermore, 28 USC §994(t) provides:

> "The Commission, promulgating general policy statements regarding the sentencing modification provisions in section 3582(c)(1)(A) of Title 18, shall describe what should be considered extraordinary and compelling reasons for sentence reduction, including the criteria to be applied and a list of specific examples. Rehabilitation of the defendant alone shall not be considered an extraordinary and compelling reason."

Several Federal District Courts around the Country have been using this avenue under the First Step Act to address unusually long sentences. A major concern with the federal courts is the defendant "age at the time" he or she committed the offense. Several Federal defendants with all types of crimes and violent offenses have been getting released. I know a bunch of individuals who had life without parole that never thought about making it out of prison alive but were granted compassionate release. They're home right now. I tried to gain some relief from the First Step Act. It didn't work.

In the petition, I argued, almost verbatim, the following: I recognize that murder is an especially heinous crime, and that the facts surrounding the offense that I was convicted of are extremely violent. I express extreme remorse for those acts. While there are understandably discrepancies between some of the evidence that was admitted at trial and what occurred from my perspective and recollection, these discrepancies in no way excuse or justify my actions with a racketeering enterprise.

Throughout, the RICO enterprise and drug trafficking conspiracy, I was under the age of 22 years old; lacked maturity, and my decision-making abilities were less developed. As a matter of fact, this was the defense's theory during trial and at the penalty phase.

Children are constitutionally different from adults for purposes of sentencing. Because juveniles have diminished culpability and greater prospects for reform... They are less deserving of the most severe punishments... First, children have a lack of maturity and an underdeveloped sense of responsibility, leading to recklessness, impulsivity, and heedless risk-taking. Second, children are more vulnerable.., to negative influences and outside pressures, including from their family and peers, they have limited control over their own environment and lack the ability to extricate themselves from horrific, crime-producing settings. And third, a child's character is not as "well formed" as an adult's; his traits are "less fixed" and his actions less likely to be evidence of irretrievable depravity.

I explained that, by legal definition, a young adult when these offenses took place, the same reasoning and scientific findings that require children be viewed differently from adults in regard to sentencing should be applied to the analysis for the bases of finding that "extraordinary and compelling reasons" for a reduction of his sentence or time-served. Moreover, I also argued that the same rationale would be or should be used to conclude to view whether or not I should be labeled a threat to the community, and future dangerousness. This all applied along with the fact that, I was only 16 years old when entering the racketeering enterprise and under the age of 22 years old when the offenses took place.

Once again I stated that, the Supreme Court opinions in Miller and Graham along with all the new scientific findings of the slow growth of a juvenile/young offenders prefrontal lope (brain) were not present back in July 2006 when I received a life without parole sentence.

In addition to presenting the young offender issue, I combined this with an argument that I had a disproportionately severe sentence compared to sentences imposed on 'Leaders of Major Drug Trafficking Organizations' and, or defendants with similar Federal offenses that's convicted of murders. I placed before the Court several illustrations of this argument:

* Diego Rodriguez and Alan Quinones ran a racketeering enterprise that focused on distribution of cocaine and heroin in Bronx, New York and elsewhere. Alan Quinones was the head of the enterprise. Rodriguez served as his chief lieutenant until

Quinones was arrested.

Rodriguez murdered a confidential informant who was blamed for Quinones arrest. The two were charged with RICO and a drug conspiracy along with murder of the confidential informant in connection with the drug trafficking. Both were convicted, in federal court, then sentenced to life.

After 20 years of imprisonment, Rodriguez was granted a reduced sentence to 30 years of imprisonment.

* Amaury Rosario was 17 when he, along with his co-defendants, shot and killed four unarmed people during a robbery gone wrong.

After two decades in prison, guards as well as inmates attested to his character and positive influence; moreover, mental-health experts working for both the defense and the prosecution at his resentencing agreed that "he had been rehabilitated and... no longer poses a significant risk to the public."

Rosario was resentenced to 28 years based on the Miller opinion by the Supreme Court.

*Osiel Carcenas-Guillen was the former head of the Gulf Cartel. The Gulf Cartel was responsible for importing thousands of kilograms of cocaine in to the United States from Mexico and using violence and intimidation to further the goals of the criminal enterprise. In 2010, Cardenas-Guillen was sentenced to 25 years in Federal prison.

*The Arellano-Felix Drug Organization("AFO") was once among the world's most violent and powerful multi-national drug trafficking organizations. The AFO was responsible for moving hundreds of tons of cocaine and marijuana from Mexico and Columbia in to the United States. The organization terrorized the Southwest United States border with executions, torture, beheadings, kidnappings, and bribes to law enforcement. In 2013, Eduardo Arellano-Felix, who acted as the chief financial officer of the organization was sentenced to 15 years in federal prison. His brother Benjamin, also an organization leader, was previously sentenced to 25 years in federal prison. The third brother and primary leader of the organization, Javier, was sentenced to life in prison.

* Antonio Guerrero was another drug dealer, involved in a drug conspiracy, that murdered two people. On April 7, 2009, a federal grand jury in the Southern District of New York returned an indictment charging, inter alia, Antonio Guerrero with the intentional murders of two while engaged in an offense punishable section 841(b)(1)(A), "to wit, a conspiracy to distribute fifty grams and more" of crack cocaine, in violation of Section 848(e)(1)(A), Title 18. After a six-week trial, Guerrero was found guilty of both charges of murder then sentenced to two concurrent terms of 25 years of imprisonment.

This motion went before the Federal Judge who sentenced me back in July of 2006. This is the process for the compassionate release/reduction of sentence motions. He denied this motion by stating that, "while this Court recognizes that Defendant had enormous obstacles and trauma to overcome and truly sympathizes with his plight, we nevertheless cannot find these circumstances warrant releasing or reducing defendant's life sentences for what were unquestionably heinous, premeditated murders of four people and other crimes. Defendant participated in the planning and fulfillment of each of those murders."

This statement was misleading by the Court. I was never convicted on four murders. But, the Court went on to state that, "Defendant may have been just 16 or 17 when he first became associated with the Boyle Street Boys, but he continued that association and the racketeering activities that went with it uninterrupted until he was arrested at age 23. Notwithstanding that more recent research may reveal that brain development in adolescents continues through the mid-20's, Mr. Cooper was one of the principal, senior members of an extremely violent criminal enterprise who was actively engaged in the planning and organization of its operations and the crimes committed in furtherance thereof -- he was not a low-level member or underling." The Court just tossed the whole scientific community research out of the window. I appealed these issues all the way up to the Third Circuit Court of Appeals which denied these issues without even given an opinion on it. The Eastern District of Pennsylvania is being extremely conservative with granting any young offenders relief pursuant to the First Step Act. Although, the Supreme Court Justice Sotomayer recently stated that, "Youth matters in sentencing." Well, youth didn't matter for us than, and still don't matter now because the Courts in the Eastern District of Pennsylvania are not setting the foundation for the lower courts to follow this understanding of youth brain development.

This is not the case with other Federal courts around the Country. These Courts are listening and abiding by the

Supreme Court decisions and research on young offenders. A number of RICO and drug conspiracy cases that have multiple violent crimes (murders) have released young offenders. Let's look at the criminal case of Luis Noel Cruz. The New Haven Register described Cruz circumstances like this, "sentenced to life in prison for killing (two individuals) as part of racketeering offenses committed while he was a member of the Latin Kings. Cruz argued that the risks posed by the coronavirus pandemic, the opportunity to care for his mother, the relative harshness of his life sentence, the possibility of his age, 18, at the time of the offense, and Cruz's "extraordinary rehabilitation" while in prison were sufficient reasons to compel (Judge) Hall to commute Cruz's sentence and compassionately release him."

The story also went on to state, "The effect is that Cruz, who was less than fully blameworthy for his crimes given his age when he committed them, will end up serving significantly more time than adults who, fully blameworthy for their conduct, have committed the same crimes." (Judge) Hall wrote in her decision. Cruz was released from federal prison after serving 26 years of incarceration for crimes that occurred in his youth. My request was denied but Cruz's request had been granted. Although, our cases have similar circumstances with each other. There's also other cases.

In the Federal Court of Appeals out of the Fourth Circuit, a panel of Judges stated that, "court's focused on the defendant's relative youth -- from 19 to 24 years old -- at the time of their offenses, a factor that many courts have found relevant under 3582(c)(1)(A)." All three co-defendants in this case decided by the Fourth Circuit were released from federal prison , even though they were convicted of violent crimes. Another Federal Court of Appeals out of the Second Circuit stated that, "Zullo's age at the time of his crime [,between 17 and 24,]... might perhaps weigh in favor of a sentence reduction." In addition to those cases, take a glance at this Federal Court out of New York which went on to declare that, "many courts have mentioned in passing that a defendant's relative youth at the time of an offense may contribute to a finding of extraordinary and compelling circumstances. But, this Court is unaware of any prior case addressing how and why an offender's youth matters to the §3582(c)(1)(i) inquiry. Given the importance of this issue to this case, however, the Court will consider it in some detail." The Court went on to break down the law, in conjunction with the First Step Act. Although, the First Step Act brought an avenue for the Court to reconsider an unusually long sentence - all of it is discretionary. You may have a better chance of hitting the lottery then getting released if you have a violent offense. Therefore, all this means is that you can beg, plead, cry, obtain a Doctorate degree from college or any other rehabilitative accomplishments, and be the best prisoner in America, if the Judge does not agree with modifying or granting a person relief then your stuck doing an unusually long sentence. This hurts young offenders who has a judge that doesn't agree that they should be given a second chance or follow the newly recognized science.

I have found one lawyer/advocate that recognizes this flaw in the legal system. The Associate Director of the University of Chicago's Federal Criminal Justice Clinic wrote in the USA Today last year and stated that, "talk is cheap, and while the administration's rhetoric is promising, second chances remain few and far between in a federal criminal system where the Department of Justice continues to thwart the administration's goals by opposing the release of individuals who are rehabilitated and do not pose a risk to the public. Making good on his commitment to criminal justice reform requires more than rhetoric. The Biden administration's Department of Justice must change course." In addition to advocating for the President to do something about criminal justice reform, Ms. Zonkel is urging Congress to take up a bill similar to D.C.'s Omnibus Public Safety and Justice Amendment Act of 2020. The compassionate release like bill for youthful offenders that committed their crimes between the ages of 18 and 25. It offers a second chance to those who made mistakes in their youth. President Biden, Department of Justice or the lawmakers have not even considered doing anything this ambition. Which is why we still have mass incarceration, and so many young offenders filling up these federal prisons with no hope and nothing to look forward too.

On a visit at FCI Cumberland with Cassie Monaco. She's a friend who has been advocating for my release.

CHAPTER 8

Unforgiven legal system

Basically, what I am trying to relay to the young offenders is that the Federal legal system is unforgiven. Especially, to young offenders that's charged with drug trafficking, racketeering and violent crimes in aid of racketeering offenses. In my personal opinion, receiving a 20-, 30-, or 40-year sentence could be your demise. I didn't even mention the death-by-incarceration sentence of life without parole. Nobody's guaranteed to make it out of federal prison or prison period. A lot of things go down in federal prisons that's not discussed in the public. Race-riots, prison riots, geographic politics over street drama, politics over prison cells, tables and televisions. The racist correctional officers that set you up to get hurt or murdered in some incidents. All of this could lead to a young offender getting murdered, seriously injured, or having to take a life of someone else. All of the above is possible in prison and would forever ruin your life.

They don't care if you're a young offender or not. If, you serve life or not. So, I wrote this book as a reminder to the young offenders to be careful. Don't rush into growing up so fast then failing by making some grave mistakes. Then after that one mistake having to go through the Federal legal system. I was arrested at 23 years old. By the type of federal charges that I received from the Government it forced me to learn the law. It's a shame that most of the people entering the Federal system never even attempt to try, at least, to learn the law, as it pertains to their case. It's a sad thing but it is the norm.

I mention this because most of the young offenders are fighting, shooting and killing to stay alive on the streets so why go to prison and just lay down. Just like your at war on the streets for whatever reasons, you should keep that mind set and go to war for your freedom in the system. And, the only way I see warring for your freedom is by learning the law. I use to read all types of law books but still didn't have a clue about what federal law was. So, I understand why some wouldn't even try but being war ready, with this mind-set, you got to at least try. It takes a long time to understand the new language of legal jargon, so I had somebody to teach me while in the Federal Detention Center in Philadelphia. The old-timer's name was Mr. Thorton.

We met in 2003 when I got sent to his unit in FDC Philly. Mr. Thorton had been arrested on bank robbery charges but still wasn't facing the same time that I was facing for racketeering charges. This wasn't his first case either. Mr. Thorton had given back 125 years on a State Racketeering charge in the State of Florida. Mr. Thorton had sat me down then explained that I needed to learn the law. Well, not learn the law but the reality about our current legal system in America. He stated that I needed to understand this foundation before he would go on to teach me anything else about federal law. This is after several months gone past when I thought that I was learning the law. What, I was learning was nothing but the basics. It was during this crucial time that I had been just handed a superseding indictment. The Government threw the whole federal criminal codes book at us. Several charges were death-qualified which meant that I was facing the Federal Death Penalty. But, I would never forget a gem that Mr. Thorton put in my head about the law. Mr. Thorton gave me a piece of paper, and he stated that this is what the law truly is. So, I read this paper, and it read like this:

"See what the law is. When these men - the rich - get control of things, they make the laws. They do not make the laws to protect anybody. Courts are not instruments of justice. When your case gets into court, it will make little difference whether you are guilty or innocent, but it's better if you have a smart lawyer. And you cannot have a smart lawyer unless you have money.

"First and last, it's a question of money. Those people who own the Earth make the laws to protect what they have. They fix up a sort of fence or pen around what they have, and the law so the fellow on the outside cannot get in. The laws are really organized for the protection of the men who rule the world. They were never organized or enforced to do justice. We have no system for doing justice, not the slightest in the world."

The words were of the famous lawyer named Charles Darrow. He lived during the late 19th and 20th century. Charles Darrow had a brilliant legal mind and used it to help the powerful, as well as the Black folks back than. It's rumored that he never lost a case. He spoke these words to a group of prisoners at the local Chicago lockup in 1902. This speech was dubbed the "Address to the Prisoners in the Cook County Jail", which caused a huge sensation at the time. These words still ring a lot of truth to this day. What system of justice would let young offenders rot in prison? When, the elite professors from the most esteemed universities around the Country stepped forward with findings from studies that our brains are not fully developed until the mid-20's. Why are Federal courts split on this issue? It doesn't make sense that the lawmakers haven't attacked this problem with young offenders receiving life sentences. Well, it does make sense if you take a look in to the fact that, most of us come from poverty-stricken upbringings. Lack the true understanding of this criminal justice system, which we're most affected by. We don't have relationships with lawyers, and most of these lawyers don't understand us or can relate to our struggles. A lot of the lawyers are part of the problem, if you really look at it. Why! They should be upholding the Constitution and protecting our rights to the fullest extent of the law. But, that is not what's going on in them courtrooms. We don't have relationships with lawyers, and don't know how to talk to them either. What I mean by relationships is that, the lawyer takes the time to know who you are personally, reads all your files, makes enough time to obtain an informed assessment of the case then gives you a fair chance in the legal proceedings. Believe me, most Black and Brown defendants have not received this type of representation. And, this problem that we're fighting with the lawyers is not a money issue. It's bigger and deeper than that. Race, status, class and the degree of wealth plays a role in the type of representation you receive. Just ask anybody who's had paid counsel, and another who's had court-appointed counsel. The two represent you the same, specifically when your Black or Brown defendants in the courtroom, and the news cameras are not rolling. Most of these lawyers come in with a preconceived notion of the facts because of the color of your skin. No matter what type of money you pay them. We don't get the same representation that others get.

Let's just take a look at this. Now, on the other hand, the rich and well-connected don't face the same problems in them courtrooms or with representation. A prime example is of the 76 year old man named Dr. John N. Kapoor. He's a former billionaire who founded opioid maker Insys Therapeutics Inc. Dr. Kapoor was sentenced to 5 years in prison for his role in a racketeering conspiracy to illegally boosting sales of his company's prescription fentanyl drug.

The Government contributed somewhere around 5 to 6 thousand fatal overdose deaths to Dr. Kapoor. He had also been indicted and convicted on federal drug charges, but the Federal District Court Judge dismissed the drug charges. This is so even after the overwhelming evidence that Dr. Kapoor knowingly and intentionally committed the crimes.

He had several co-defendants cooperate with the Government and broke down the whole drug conspiracy and racketeering enterprise. During, Dr. Kapoor's, sentencing seven victims or their family members spoke about the harm they suffered from Subsys, from lost teeth to the death of a loved one to the drug. The prosecutors sought only 15 years for Dr. Kapoor, but the Federal District Court Judge settled on only 5 years of imprisonment. Dr. Kapoor was convicted with four other former Insys executives and managers. One of those convicted had ran an escort service. Dr. Kapoor used women, and other things to bribe treating physicians to boost sales of the fentanyl drug. This tactic was used so that the physicians could over-prescribe the doses of the fentanyl. Nobody received a life without parole sentence, twenty year sentence or anything over the five year sentence. Dr. Kapoor got the harshest sentence because he was the leader of this operation or enterprise.

How could this be that, young offenders can receive a life without parole for only one fatal shooting. Yet, Dr. Kapoor gets attributed thousands of deaths and receives only a five-year sentence. Which, he may not even be serving because of appealing the sentence and released on an appeal bond. Dr. Kapoor was out on bail fighting the federal charges along with the other co-defendants who went to trial.

Now, there is some clear injustice going on here. Nobody raised hell about this sentence. Nobody raised hell about the sentencing disparities that Blacks and Browns face when charged, convicted and sentenced on similar racketeering conduct. Here's a rich and powerful man who benefited from the system because of his status and wealth along with superior legal representation.

With examples like this, how can there be any arguments against reducing young offenders' sentences all around the federal system. I am talking about young offenders with a federal offense that took place before their 23rd birthday. That is what "real justice" would provide for young offenders. It's not, as though we don't have evidence to back our mitigating factors up that supports less than life without parole sentences for young offenders.

It is clear that they want to wipe our names out of history. Well, better yet, place you in history with the worst decision you ever made as a young offender, and let that define for future generations about the person you were. No, they don't want to give you a chance to redeem yourself. A chance to apologize to the victims of your crimes. A chance to apologize to your family. A chance to show society that you changed and reformed yourself. A chance to write a different ending for yourself, and family.

Everybody deserves a second chance, if they reformed and rehabilitated their actions and thinking. Which, I think a person can do after spending 20 years in prison for any crime. I stand by this even for those that, we, think is less deserving for any chance. People get older, mature, and change all the time.

So, my advice to the teenagers or young offenders growing up is to slow down. Stop trying to grow up so fast. Enjoy your parents, friends and other relatives because life is short and they're not always going to be here. Taking a life isn't right except if it's for self-defense. Losing your life to prison is serious. There's nothing fun, cool or thrill about serving a life without parole sentence or any type of prison sentence. Coming to prison in your 20's then growing old to graying while in prison. Or go from becoming a young and immature offender to turning into a mature man or woman through incarceration. What about the fact of raising your kids from a prison phone. Receiving the news of losing a loved one from death through a federal prison phone system. Or being delivered the news of a loved one death from a prison chaplain. Life is real. Lost is real for all parties involved. Your life matters. We're not taught that our lives matter. Maybe this could be the reason why its so easy for us to ruin other people lives. We're not told that your special and have a purpose in this world. I think it's also because we're raised next to them corner Stop signs, in them drug infested neighborhoods and surrounded by nothing but hate. Being lead by those so-called Ol'Heads that don't know no better.

The lames that's leading us down the wrong paths in life. Having you put the work in that they're scared to do. Yeah, the same lames who don't visit you, send money or even check on a few of your loved ones while you're in prison.

My thing is that don't believe them that prison or death is all that you can get or choose to look forward too. The times are different. The people are different. The world is different. We got to understand that life is about choices. Although, most if not all of us, never have all the information to make informed decisions about our lives but we got to strive to get informed. One way of getting informed is by reading and learning about the failures of others. Learn from the mistakes of people like me. Learn from the failings and short comings of the others that I've mentioned in this book or from any of the people that you looked up to in life but failed and went to prison. Selling drugs and committing violent crimes, no matter how young you are, or how isolated the crimes are from your homies or neighborhood or group or gang; all of this can land you in federal prison serving a hefty sentence. Maybe even serving a life without parole sentence. And, when your laying up in a tiny freezing federal prison cell looking in the mirror by the day and getting old and gray by the night along with serving whatever lengthy sentence that you received and see how hard it is to get out from under that sentence -- I warned you right here.

Receiving any equal justice is so hard to get. Don't think by a long shot that it can't happen to you because it can. I use to think the same way. Well, the evidence that I got convicted on was co-defendant testimony. Several cooperating witnesses for the Government that I won't name because it doesn't even matter at this point in life. No citizen witnesses stated that I committed any violent act. It was only so-called friends. But the Federal Government took down the best of them. Believe me because I have been around most of them through these 19 years of incarceration and helping them with their legal struggles trying to get out of prison.

At the end of the day, go ahead and make that transition. The transition from the streets is always the hardest part but change is always hard. Maturing and thinking for yourself takes time and discipline for some to do. But I suggest that any money that you've obtained so far, invest it in your education or any other type of hustle that you can do that's legit. Better yet, make somebody else life better. A family member, friend or stranger. Do something with the money, and your talents before it's to late. If not, you will be spending it on lawyers who don't care for you or your kind, commissary and all the other things that costs so much to survive and live comfortably in federal prison serving an unusually long sentence. People may say I changed after reading this book, but I beg to differ. I just call it MATURITY.

LETTER FROM CO-DEFENDANT-JAMAIN WILLIAMS

Subject:

How Rico Laws is being use in the Black Community.

My name is Jamain Williams from Chester, PA. 19013

I have been sentence to 3 life consecutive sentences following a rico convictions.

This law was created for the purpose of the Mafia and Organize Enterprise doing illegal activities, not kids in poor neighborhoods that grew up in tight-nit community.

Growing up in the neighborhood whereas it nothing but crime and nothing really positive to do, I was lead into selling drugs at a young age. At an early age, I always had a vision to make money to get out of the hood and move out of Chester for a better life. School at that time really was hard and the teachers really didn't take an interest in a single individual learning skills. (SMH)

You know what funny? When I was young, I always didn't like drug dealers. I thought they was the worst people or something. Guess that come from me watching TV and my mom always preaching that to us at an early age. So my ambition was to become a lawyer or doctor or something. But for some reasoning, I couldn't learn as fast as I wanted to. However, when I started leaving my street and started hanging around the older guys, they didn't seem that bad and I thought it was cool. Shoot, the good people seem like; the ones selling drugs was cool and the cops; that never spoke, was the ones that looked hateful. (SMH).

My first time getting locked-up for drugs. I think I was around 13 or 14 years old. I was standing watching the older guy playing basketball in the streets and out of nowhere everybody said "cops! Narc!" One of the drug dealers said "Jay, hold this." He took my hand and placed bag of drugs in my hand and said nothing. I'd put them in my pocket and tried to walk away but the cop put me down and found the drugs. At the time I was so in shock and scare, I didn't even talk until my Mom came to pick me up. After I'd got out of jail, the old head end up giving me 20 dollar for keepin my mouth shut. Once again, I was hurt. This dude didn't even apologize and after all that, gave me $20.

That right there showed me drug dealers are not crack up what they act like. So I really hated or didn't want to sell drugs. But now how do I move on from that. I couldn't figure that out. Tried school, but it was hard. Nobody to talk to and explain about life. The only people that really told me I could be something was the dope boys.

So now I had started selling drugs on my own.

Growing up in Highland Gardens we never experience gangs. Actually that was like a no-no in our hood. It's like everybody sold drugs for theirself. Back then I always seen everybody just running to cars and whoever dive through window got the sales. (SMH) So I guess, we started emulating the samething also. Me and all the kids that hung around neighborhood. Every man for hisself when making money. I mean, growing up in the neighborhood, not once had we see any type of gang where it was a leader or somebody calling the shots and everybody listen. I think nobody knew what even was a Shot-Caller, Big Homie was back then. Mafia we only saw on

TV and movie (lol) But giving another man an order was laughed at.
Man, being locked-up on a Rico law is crazy for me. Yeah, I made mistakes when I was young I wish I had somebody to explain what we was getting ourselves into just being around somebody or ya friends while doing crime can affect you also. But being label as a gang is the worst thing in our hood. It's like, being a follower for something that don't make since. Fighting over the clothes you wear or the colors. I'd hated that type of image

I wish I could explain it to the young kids in our old neighborhood about how the Feds is using this rico law that got nothing to do with organized crime but using it against young black males to incarcerate; danwear on other people crime. Or testimony. (Smh) It's like, after you get charge with that rico law there is no way anybody in the black community can get found not guilty. I wish I could really sit down with the young guys and explain to them how the system work against and let them know it are life out there in the world where you could live a successful life without selling drugs. I mean, it so many avenue out there to make money where you don't have to work really hard. Even though it hard for some kid to learn in school, it jobs out there that you can still use you skills on being honest and want to change in your life. I wish I could tell the young dudes that. Especially my son.

Being incarcerated for 20years I had the time to think about the crimes I had done and ask myself "Was it worth it?" Hell No! Only if I coulda told my young self that or anybody sat me down and explain that, I wouldn't made alot of mistakes.

Hopefully while I am still young, I could reach out to kids and hopefully change their life because some of them can still be save from that street life.

Sincerely Yours
Jamain Williams.

ONLINE POST FROM FRIEND AND ADVOCATE - CASSIE MONACO

ANDRE COOPER JUVENILE LIFER

Updated Mar 19. 2020

Recently I went to visit Andre Cooper at FCI Cumberland. Andre contacted me last May from an Op-ed published in the Washington Examiner. My Op-ed dealt with white-collar offenses, and Andre is a Juvenile lifer .

Andre and I have been communicating through email since May. His story compelled me to try and help him. It was a calling I could not deny or shake. Andre was charged with 'Violent Crimes in Aid of Racketeering' federal charge - 18 USC 1959(a)(1). A charge with which I am unfamiliar.

The grounds of FCI Cumberland are quite pleasant. The facility is surrounded by Walls. Mountain and Haystack mountain in Western Maryland. An abundance of mature trees give this place almost a serene setting, and I quickly noticed how eerily quiet it was there. I sat in my car for a moment to look up Andre's BOP number, so I would have it to write on the required visitation form. I felt a deep ache in my chest, and sadness as his release date stated LIFE. I thought to myself if I have this type of reaction, not even having met this man yet how he must have felt hearing the judge hand him a life sentence and what heartache and despair his mother felt

FCI Cumberland has a medium facility along with a camp. I have been visiting my husband for three and a half years at a Federal camp in Denver. I quickly learned that the procedure for a medium facility is much more intimidating. The first thing the correctional officers said to me as I pulled open the glass door with zest and entered the lobby, "You must be looking for the camp." I was taken aback by why they would make that assumption. I said, "No, I am where I need to be." I walked to the table that held the required visitation forms. It felt somewhat odd as It has become so routine to fill out these forms with my husband's information, and today I was filling it out with another person's information. I thought I had come very preparedly for visiting as I had learned the rules from visiting my husband. The dollar bills I had in my clear baggie that are acceptable when visiting my husband are not allowed here. I ***had*** *to change the dollars into coins at the change machine before going was a no go; The officer was polite in telling me he would keep it for me after he made a joke if there was enough money on the card to do some online* *shopping. They asked for my car key and then handed me a silver token. I wondered aloud what it was for they told me when I bring it back after visiting, they would give me back my key.*

I then put my coat, shoes, and clear baggie, which now contains dollar coins on the x-ray machine. I walked through the metal detector without incident. I came prepared as i had often heard from other ladies to wear a sports bra because an underwire bra will set off the alarm, and you won't be allowed to enter visiting. I put back on my shoes and coat, which the officers allowed me to take with me and then stamped my hand with invisible ink. One of the officers asked me to come behind the desk. He swabbed my hands with gauze and said he was testing for drugs, and he let me know this was routine. My mind raced for a minute as I had heard of people testing positive because they had just pumped gas in their car. I thought for a moment had I filled up with gas, and I realized I had not. The machine beeped I had passed the test.

One of the officers was now my escort to visiting. We went through one set of doors which lead to a hallway, and the left wall was blacked out glass. I was told to put my hand that was now home to invisible ink under a scanner, and once I heard a knock on the window, I could proceed. I looked at the officer in a confused manner and asked if someone was behind the glass. The answer was yes. I heard a loud two knocks and the officer, and I continued our walk. At the end of the hallway, he unlocked the door that leads to the outside. We walked across the courtyard, and again I take notice of how quiet it is not a good quiet but an unsettling stillness.

I was led into visiting by the officer opening yet another locked door. The officer behind the visiting desk asked who I was there to see. The officer then instructed me on which set of plastic tables and chairs I would sit. I promptly took my seat and then told I need to sit on the chair on the other side of the table. I was perplexed for a moment until I observed that there are specific sides for the residents and visitors to sit.

Sitting waiting for Andre, I observed everyone visiting. The couple next to me enjoying their vending machine lunch while capturing life and intimacy in laughter. An older white man was visiting a black man. They had shaken hands not like they were life long friends but more like new friends. A woman with three restless children was visiting her; I assumed husband. It was a calm visiting room I took note of how respectful everyone was and again the quiet even though half of the room is filled with people.

I recognized Andre from his photo on his change.org petition. A black man standing about 5'10 bald head, beard, and institution glasses. I stood we said hello, and he extended his hand for a handshake I instead opted to greet him with a hug. We exchanged pleasantries. He said he wasn't sure that I would visit today. I smiled and said that it was my mission to come and visit him today and how happy I was to be there. I thought to myself that it must be a coping skill not to have expectations to avoid disappointment.

Although Andre wrote to me his story, I wanted to be able to grasp his words and feel his emotions by him telling me his story sitting across from me. He began by telling me his mother was fifteen years old when she gave birth to Andre. He was born in Wilmington, His father stayed in Wilmington.

Andre explains to me that Chester was and still is a dangerous place to live. With no parental supervision, he started running the streets at twelve years old and smoking weed at thirteen. Andre was abducted thrown into a trunk of a car and pistol-whipped at the age of fourteen. He thought his life was over that day. His uncle taught him to sell drugs, and without Andre having any mentor looking out for him and growing up in an impoverished, violent, and drug-infested neighborhood, he was in constant survival mode. His mentors and idols became the drug dealers who were driving the new Mercedes, dressed in designer clothing and dripping of expensive watches and jewelry. Dealing drugs was the *business that Andre knew and for which he was being groomed. To Andre, those men driving the Mercedes in his impoverished neighborhood were what he perceived as being a success.*

Andre started his story with what he was charged with racketeering. I did not know what racketeering is I had heard the term I thought it had something to do with illegal gambling. I asked Andre what it meant in layman's terms. He said it is what they would charge the mafia within organized crime, The following is the definition. Racketeering is a criminal activity in which a person or organization engages in a "racket." A racket is when the criminal creates a problem for others for the purpose of solving that problem by some type of extortion. The person or organization who engages in the racket is called a racketeer. Andre was 16 years old at the start of this alleged racketeering and cocaine(drug) trafficking enterprise. Federal prosecutors alleged that Andre and his codefendants formed an association or drug enterprise called "The Boyle Street Boys." These kids were all seventeen and younger and lived in the same neighborhood hence the name that the prosecutors gave to their alleged organization.

I had stopped Andre for a moment to offer him something to eat and drink from the vending machines. He was a bit shy in accepting my offer. I insisted as I know all too well what lack of quality food is fed to the men and women who are incarcerated. It is a luxury to have an opportunity to eat real food if even that food comes from a vending machine. At least it is not marked "Not for human consumption."

As I come back to sit down with an assortment of snacks, we pick up where we left off with our conversation, I had to lean in close to hear Andre again the quiet. Everyone in the room spoke in a low voice. There were three homicides included in Andre and his codefendant's indictment. Andre's convictions include the aiding and abetting of two of the killings and the hand that pulled the trigger on the third victim. The third victim that Andre is charged in killing is a man that murdered Andre's cousin. I asked Andre if he had done it if he had pulled the trigger. He was not defensive of me asking the question. What I felt from him and what I saw was a moment of reliving a life that has long passed him a life that he could no longer imagine. What I saw was remorse and thoughts of what could have been had he the opportunity.

Andre wanted to know about me. I shared with him some of my life stories He was surprised I did not attend college. He said, You could never tell." I spoke about my husband Chris and his journey and what a romantic and good man he is. I talked about how I had run away at the age of seventeen. I enjoyed seeing him genuinely laugh. I gave them the examples of resident vs. inmate, returning citizen vs offender. He laughed and said, "no, Cassie, we don't use that language in here.' It was as though our conversation had just begun when I heard the CO yell INMATES against the wall, and visitors stay seated I was startled and said, what happened? Andre said everything is okay visiting is just over I was irked that visiting had to end in such a harsh manner, I found it unnecessary. We parted our visit the same way we had begun with a hug.

Visitors remained seated until the section we were sitting was called to leave. We were escorted out by a correctional officer. Half-way across the courtyard was a sign that said visitors stop here until motioned to continue As I stood looking at that sign along with four other ladies, the cold wind whipping causing a frigid coldness all I could think is I would suck at being an incarcerated person. Conforming at such a high level is unnatural.

There were many moments during our visit where I teared up and had to hold back from crying. Andre grew up in Federal Prison he is now a man who sits before me with gray in his beard, and he entered the system as a very young man. During our visit, he looked at me, and he spoke with such conviction and passion. Telling me Cassie, I am not that person I was as a boy I am reformed, I reformed myself. The prison system is not going to reform anyone: you have to choose to become a better person and to grow, and I made that choice.

In the letter that Andre sent me eight months ago, the very first sentence reads. I am not proud of some of the things that I've done, took part in. or which I am accused of. I'm truly remorseful and sorry for the pain that I've caused a lot of people in the community. Andre was transparent in his letter to me, leaving out no details in his honesty. He ended the letter saying Cassie; I had been changing my life well-before the juvenile or young adult issues were coming to light. Everything that I stated in this email, I can provide proof of it to you I hope this helps and don't view me in a different light because of the facts of my case. But I had to be upfront with you about the facts of my life and situation.

I see Andre as a man that as a boy had made some awful decisions. Andre was just a boy at the time. and his environment dictated a lot of his behavior, I have not walked in Andre's shoes. I do not know what it is like to have to survive in a neighborhood full of violence, drugs, and poverty. What I do know is that this man, along with many other juvenile lifers, deserves a second chance. They deserve an opportunity at life. What gifts we are missing out on that these people could bring into our world if we just recognized them now as grown men and women, not the children they once were.

https://www.adaycloser.org/post/andre-cooper-juvenile-lifer

Sources

1. www.chestercity.com
2. African American Organized Crime: A Social History, By Rufus Schatzberg and Robert J. Kelly
3. United States v. Nacrelli, 468 F. Supp. 241(3rd Cir. 1979)
4. United States v. West, 508 F. Supp. 1028(3rd Cir. 1981)
5. United States v. Anderson, 1987 U.S. Dist. LEXIS 1764(3rd Cir. 1987)
6. United States v. Scarfo, 850 F.2d 1015(3rd Cir. 1988)
7. United States v. Eufrasio, 935 F.2d 553(3rd Cir. 1990)
8. United States v Thomas, 114 F.3d 228(D.C. Cir. 1997)
9. The Prosecution of Sophisticated Urban Street Gangs: A Proper Application of RICO, By Lesley Suzanne Bonney, Catholic University Law review (1993)
10. American Bar Association: Death Penalty Due Process Review Project Section of Civil Rights and Social Justice, By Seth Miller and Robert Weiner (2018)
11. In re Andre Williams, 759 F.3d 66(D.C. Cir. 2014)

12. In re Thomas F. Hoffner, Jr., 870 F.3d 301(3rd Cir. 2017)
13. Andre Cooper, Who's Going To Save Us (2019)
14. United States v. Barbeito, 2010 U.S. Dist. LEXIS 55688(4th Cir.)
15. Andre Cooper, Are You A Racketeer? (2020)
16. United States v. Roy, 855 F.3d 1153(11th Cir. 2017)
17. www.cnn.com/joeligon/
18. United States Sentencing Commission, Youthful Offenders in the Federal System (2017)
19. www.usatoday.com
20. United States v. Wirsing, 943 F.3d 175(4th Cir. 2019)
21. New Haven Register Newspaper
22. United States v. Cruz, 2021 U.S. Dist. LEXIS 68857(2nd Cir.)
23. United States v. Rodriguez, 2020 U.S Dist. LEXIS 181004(2nd Cir.)
24. United States v. Simon, 2021 U.S. App. LEXIS 25591 (1st Cir.)
25. www.nytimes.com
26. BNA INsights 90 Crim. L. Rep. (BNA) 280 November 23, 2011, By Glen Austin By Glen Austin Sproviero

27. The Meaning of Life, Marc and Ashley Nellis
28. What We Know, Edited Vivian Nixon and Daryl V. Atkinson
29. United States v. Rosario, 2018 US Dist. LEXIS 134657(2nd. Cir.)
30. Osiel Carcenas-Guillen, Former Head of the Gulf Cartel, sentenced to 25 years' imprisonment, available at https://www.fbi.gov/houston/press-releases/2010/ho022410b.htm
31. Last of the Arellano-Felix Brothers Sentenced (Aug. 19, 2013), available at https://www.fbi.gov/sandiego/press-releases/2013/last-of-the-arellano-flex-brothers-sentenced
32. United States v. Guerrero, 813 F.3d 462(2nd Cir. 2016)
33. Jailhouse Lawyers, By Mumia Abu-Jamal
34. Wa11Street Journal... wsj.com/johnkapoor
35. Life without parole is wrong even if kids kill, by Austin Sarat
36. Williams v. United States, 2018 U.S. Dist. LEXIS 230463(2nd Cir.)

37. 37. Pike v. Gross, 2019 US App. LEXIS 25063(6th Cir.)

38. Micklus v. Carlson, 632 F.2d 227(3rd Cir.)

39. The Next Step: Ending Excessive Punishment for Violent Crimes, By Nazgol Ghandnoosh, Ph.D

40. United States v Edmond, 52 F.3d 1245(3rd Cir.)

OTHER TITLE BY ANDRE "DRE" COOPER

BULLIED

A Story About How A Few Teenagers Started A Movement

Please go on Amazon.com and give a review

Made in the USA
Middletown, DE
02 July 2024

56582370R00086